"Developing Multicultural Leaders provides a concise synthesis of the leadership literature while adding a unique multicultural perspective. Based on field research, this book is a valuable and insightful guide for anyone who has the desire and determination to embark on the journey to leadership success."

– Said T. Khoury
Co-founder, Chairman and President
Consolidated Contractors Company

"Developing Multicultural Leaders provides fresh insights for our work of leading a multicultural organization within the United Nations, where we function in a complex context with multiple, diverse and sometimes overlapping cultures from all over the globe. It unpacks this complexity and provides new understandings of how management, leadership and culture interact. The book examines leadership not only from Western models, but from leadership principles and practices as developed in various regions of the South. The focus on the Middle East is welcomed and long overdue."

–Thoraya A. Obaid, PhD
Executive Director, United Nations (retired)
Population Fund (UNFPA)
Under-Secretary-General of the United Nations

"It is very edifying to finally see the Middle East receiving the kind of attention it warrants by leadership scholars. The authors have done us a real service by systematically presenting, analyzing and integrating their study's findings with an impressive array of established leadership concepts. The book also has a strong practical edge for aspiring leaders who seek to lead within and beyond the Middle Eastern region."

–Brad Jackson
Professor of Leadership
Fletcher Building Education Trust Chair in Leadership
The University of Auckland Business School, New Zealand

"Developing Multicultural Leaders is an insightful study of how leaders are shaped from childhood to becoming successful heads of their organizations. CEOs and HR professionals will find, as I have, the leadership journey and the three stages of leadership development particularly relevant when viewed from the authors' multicultural, contextual, and situational perspective."

–Faisal M. Al-Suwaidi
Former Chairman and CEO
Qatargas Operating Company Limited, Qatar

"This is a breakthrough book—an invaluable guide for any global organization doing work in the Middle East or elsewhere. Cultural sensitivity is critical in today's business environment to ensure sustainable success, yet so many expatriates choose to ignore it. Were there a pyramid of success in a global organization, this competency belongs at its base."

–Paul F. Boulos, PhD
President and Chief Operating Officer
MWH Soft, Inc., US

"Farid Muna and Ziad Zennie have written a book of the utmost importance that must be read by anyone who wishes to understand what leadership is going to have to be like in the emerging realities of multicultural management. Muna's pioneering work on the Arab executive illustrated his sensitivity to countervailing trends to the prevailing Western influenced models of leadership that still dominate our narrow-focus, silo-based teaching in Business Schools. With this book, he and his colleagues have spelled out the elements of a new paradigm."

–David Weir
Professor of Intercultural Management, and Head of
Business School, Liverpool Hope University, UK
Affiliate Professor, Ecole Superieure de
Commerce, Rennes, France

"I strongly recommend reading *Developing Multicultural Leaders*. Dr. Muna and Dr. Zennie and the Meirc team have firsthand experience of developing successful leaders in the Middle East that is conveyed to the reader in this breakthrough book. Their insights on the cultural aspects of leadership will motivate managers to achieve success through sustainable development of human capital."

–Mustafa Al Sayed, PhD
Secretary-General, Royal Charity Organization, Bahrain
Former CEO of Bahrain Petroleum Company (Bapco)

"I found this book intriguing. It is also easy to read and provides an excellent guide for aspiring leaders, professionals, and entrepreneurs who manage across multicultural organizations like mine. The authors expertly map the key development stages of leadership with unique references to an important region of the world."

–Amer Salem
Co-founder, CommVerge Solutions
President, Philippines and Singapore

"Farid Muna and Ziad Zennie have compiled an insightful, empirical journey into the realm of cultural differences and sensitivity, and the importance of becoming a learner of other ways of thinking and working in multinational business contexts. Each one of the authors became literally '*Mu'allmi*,' my teacher. I invite you to join their class for improved self-awareness and performance in Middle Eastern environments of all types."

–Fenwick W. English
R. Wendell Eaves Distinguished Professor of
Educational Leadership School of Education,
University of North Carolina at Chapel Hill, US

"In *Developing Multicultural Leaders*, Muna and Zennie provide significant insights into those factors most important to leadership with a special view to their application in the Middle East. They correctly underscore the special importance of the effective 'multicultural leader' and provide specific guidance on how individuals and organizations can strengthen their multicultural leadership effectiveness."

–Ahmad S. Al-Nassar
Vice President, Management Services (retired)
Saudi Aramco, Saudi Arabia

"It is rare to read a book on leadership that deals with the vital dimension of culture and even rarer to see women interviewed in the research sample. Farid Muna and Ziad Zennie offer us both in a highly readable format. Taken together with Muna's and Meirc's other research, aptly summarized herein, this book opens wider windows on management in a critical part of the world."

– Susan Vinnicombe OBE
Professor of Organizational Behaviour and
Diversity Management, School of Management,
Cranfield University, UK

Developing Multicultural Leaders

The Journey to Leadership Success

New Edition

Farid A. Muna
Chairman of Meirc Training & Consulting
and

Ziad A. Zennie
Partner with Meirc Training & Consulting

Foreword by Charles Handy

First published 2010 by
New edition published 2011 by
PALGRAVE MACMILLAN

Palgrave Macmillan in the UK is an imprint of Macmillan Publishers Limited,
registered in England, company number 785998, of Houndmills, Basingstoke,
Hampshire RG21 6XS.

Palgrave Macmillan in the US is a division of St Martin's Press LLC,
175 Fifth Avenue, New York, NY 10010.

Palgrave Macmillan is the global academic imprint of the above companies
and has companies and representatives throughout the world.

Palgrave® and Macmillan® are registered trademarks in the United States,
the United Kingdom, Europe and other countries.

ISBN 978–0–230–31423–8   hardback

This book is printed on paper suitable for recycling and made from fully
managed and sustained forest sources. Logging, pulping and manufacturing
processes are expected to conform to the environmental regulations of the
country of origin.

A catalogue record for this book is available from the British Library.

A catalog record for this book is available from the Library of Congress.

10 9 8 7 6 5 4 3 2 1
20 19 18 17 16 15 14 13 12 11

Printed and bound in Great Britain by
CPI Antony Rowe, Chippenham and Eastbourne

Dedicated to the four ladies in my life
My wife Doris
and
Our three daughters
Rima, Nadia, and Zeina

Farid A. Muna

To my wife Jausianne
and
Our two aspiring leaders,
Our daughters
Tamara and Lara

Ziad A. Zennie

Contents

List of Figures and Boxes

List of Tables

xi

Foreword by Charles Handy

How pleasing it is to read a book on leadership that does not spring from America or Western Europe, with all the in-built cultural assumptions that inevitably follow. As the title of this book emphasizes, the world is multicultural now and the 12 countries of the Middle East that are covered by its research are too little studied and too little understood by the rest of the world yet are increasingly important.

How pleasant, too, to read a research study that starts with no preconceived theories but goes straight to the leaders themselves to ask what made them who they are, which competencies they feel they needed to get where they are, and what it is that makes the best of them outstanding as leaders. It is comforting that the study reinforces my own feeling that one cannot teach leadership, only grow potential leaders, and that the growth process starts early, in the home in fact, and is a continuing mix of education, experience, mentors and models.

It is an important book. When I worked at the London Business School I had a colleague who specialized in improving the work of groups in organizations. He left to start up and run a restaurant. I met him again a year or two later and suggested that he must be enjoying putting his ideas into practice. "You know something," he said, "I have found out that if you get the right people to start with you don't need all that stuff that I used to teach." Of course that begged the crucial question "how do you know who are the right people?" This book would have been a great help to him, and to very many like him.

One of the book's underlying premises is that culture makes a difference, that what works for leaders in one culture may not prove so successful in another. This premise was tested by a subsequent study, one in which 76 Lebanese executives, now working in Lebanon, the Gulf or the USA, were interviewed to see whether they adapted their styles of leadership to fit the new cultures. This later study, summarized in this new edition of the book, suggests that the successful leaders did indeed adapt their ways to the new host cultures, but to do that you need to know the characteristics of that culture, the sort of things that this book spells out for the countries of the Middle East.

I had the privilege of first meeting Farid Muna 35 years ago when he was studying for his doctorate at the London Business School. I subsequently acted as one of the advisers to the study undertaken by him and his organization, Meirc, titled *The Making of Gulf Managers*. I was impressed then by his desire to base the training and consultancy work of the organization on a full and proper understanding of the circumstances and needs of the managers with whom they were dealing.

This book builds on and extends that original work. It is a model of its kind and leads me to hope that it will be replicated by similar studies in other fast developing countries such as China, India and Brazil. It is probable that the formative processes for potential leaders in these countries will differ both from each other and from the established Western models. As the Lebanese study suggests, leaders and managers who change countries in the course of their careers will need to learn the ways and values of their new host cultures if they are to succeed. As more and more businesses encourage their executives to be prepared to move around the globe, both they and the executives themselves would be well advised to read this book, and others that might follow from it.

For personal reasons I hope that this book attracts many readers and sells many copies. Let me explain. Last year my wife, a portrait photographer, and I were asked by Oxfam, the British charity, to document in words and portraits, one of the early fruits of their new social venture capital fund. This fund, called the Enterprise Development Programme, was set up to invest in small enterprises in the developing world, preferably women's co-operatives and usually in agriculture. The aim was to help them grow into sustainable medium sized businesses, giving employment and a better lifestyle to more people, especially women. The enterprise that they asked us to visit was The New Farm Company in the Occupied Palestinian Territories which, as it happened, was itself an example of how the leaders learnt to go with the grain of the surrounding culture. The results of our work were exhibited in eight locations in Britain and in a booklet. More details of the project and the Enterprise Development

Programme can be found by following this link https://www.oxfam.org.uk/edp

This project has interested many people. Among them is Farid Muna who was born in Jerusalem. He and his co-author have very generously donated a large proportion of their future earnings from this book to Oxfam, to go directly to support the work of the Enterprise Development Programme. Oxfam, as well as my wife and myself, are very grateful to them for their philanthropic gesture. Once again, I hope that they can be a model for others, in this case other authors, who might be encouraged to donate a proportion of their book earnings to such charitable causes.

Charles Handy
London

Acknowledgments

Many individuals and organizations deserve credit for their significant contributions to this book. We are grateful to the 310 leaders we interviewed for this research, who gave generously of their time and effort; their cooperation made this research possible. As promised, their names will remain anonymous. We are greatly indebted to the 129 organizations, from 12 Middle Eastern countries, which identified and nominated those successful leaders.

A special note of thanks and appreciation is due to the Meirc Training & Consulting research team members who shared with us the pleasant but demanding task of interviewing the 310 leaders. They are (in alphabetical order):

Fuad W. Awad
Alex-Ameer F. Ayoub
Fadi R. Chahrouri
Alaa Elbaz
Hanna M. El-Jor
Yousef K. Gaspard
Ahmad M. Rashid
Maher A. Rayes

Many thanks go to our colleague Aiman Sadeq for his assistance with the data analyses. We are thankful to Yvonne Frank for her administrative support. We are grateful to Rima Muna for drawing the competency iceberg (Figure 6.1).

We benefited from our Meirc partners and colleagues through the lively discussions we had over the years on the topic of leadership. We acknowledge with thanks the authors of the books and articles whose work we have reviewed, and who are noted in the References section at the end of the book. We are also grateful for all those people who knowingly or unknowingly influenced our thinking on this important subject. They are too many to mention by name.

Ted Abdo (Board Member and former Chairman) and Ramsey Hakim (Board Member and Deputy Chairman) deserve special mention for their enthusiastic support for this research project. Both wholeheartedly agreed with us that, despite the global recession, this research is an investment for the future.

Finally, we are most grateful to Charles Handy for writing the Foreword to this new edition of the book. Charles, a prolific writer who is repeatedly ranked among the top management thinkers in the world, continues to inspire us with his deeds and thoughts.

Farid A. Muna, Chairman of the Board
Meirc Training & Consulting
Dana Point, California, US

Ziad A. Zennie, Partner
Meirc Training & Consulting
Dubai, United Arab Emirates

About the Authors

Farid A. Muna is Chairman of the Board of Directors at Meirc Training & Consulting. He joined Meirc in 1973 after working with an American company for several years in California and Texas. He was the Managing Director of Meirc from 1991 to 1997. His areas of interest are leadership, strategy, human resource (HR) management, and finance. He has conducted seminars in the US, Europe, the Middle East, Africa and Japan. Farid was the director and author of a major Meirc research study titled *The Making of Gulf Managers*. He has published several articles on leadership, HR, and work–life balance. In addition, he is the author of *The Arab Executive* and *Seven Metaphors on Management*.

Dr. Farid A. Muna can be reached at faridmuna@att.net.

Ziad A. Zennie is a partner with Meirc Training & Consulting, a leading management consultancy firm in the Middle East. Ziad began his career as an educator at various institutions in Lebanon. Later, he served as Assistant Principal of the training centers with a major oil company in Saudi Arabia, and as Director of a HR firm in Lebanon. In the US, Ziad was a management and educational consultant for a number of companies and schools. More recently, he has been engaged in management training for regional and multinational companies in the Middle East.

Dr. Ziad A. Zennie can be reached at zzennie@meirc.com.

Introduction

I keep six honest serving-men
(They taught me all I knew);
Their names were What and Why and When
And How and Where and Who.

— *Rudyard Kipling*

What makes great organizational leaders? This question has been asked by management thinkers, scholars, and practitioners from a multitude of countries and cultures. *Developing Multicultural Leaders* aims to answer this question using a multicultural approach and field research conducted in 12 countries.

However, to discover what makes great leaders, it is necessary to delve further and deeper and to tackle the following five related questions:

- What influence do early childhood years have on success?
- What are the specific life experiences that contribute to leadership success?
- How do leaders with potential become outstanding?
- What critical paths must leaders follow on their journey to success?
- And, finally, what must great leaders do exceptionally well to become and remain outstanding?

This book synthesizes the best leadership literature while introducing a multicultural perspective as it addresses these questions. The lessons

1

are useful for current and aspiring leaders and for those in charge of recruiting, supporting, and developing them who must take into account nuances, similarities, and differences in context and cultures. *Developing Multicultural Leaders* is about becoming a more effective and successful leader. It seeks to enrich our understanding of the ingredients for leadership and to shed light on the journey to success.

We believe that there are a number of paths on the journey to leadership success and that learning to become an outstanding leader is possible for all who are ready to put in concerted effort and have the determination to do so. This book introduces a new framework for understanding leadership. Our field research:

- Examines the early years of potential leaders (when, where, and how potential leaders acquire their abilities, skills, and attitudes),
- Looks into the competencies that potential leaders must learn and master to become outstanding (what leadership competencies are necessary for success), and
- Explores the leadership styles and action areas that outstanding leaders focus on (who succeeds, and why some leaders are more successful than others).

The practical implications of our field research are enormous. CEOs, senior executives, and human resources professionals will find important recommendations on how best to recruit, select, assess, develop, and motivate future managers and leaders not only by using competency-based approaches but also by taking into consideration those ingredients that we found to be essential for success. Moreover, this book looks at leadership from a multicultural perspective—in recognition that more large organizations are becoming more multicultural in their outlook, practices, and people, even when they do not cross national borders.

Our firm, Meirc Training & Consulting (Meirc), has been conducting management research since the early 1960s. Our vision is to continue this tradition into the twenty-first century—research which, we believe, will ultimately be of great benefit to organizations and to future leaders in the Middle East as well as other parts of the world. Over the years, participants in our senior management seminars have constantly wondered why the majority of the leadership models, concepts, and theories are based on research conducted in the West. Many of these participants continue to raise the same question today. In fact, more than 90 percent of the literature on leadership reflects US-based research and theory, with hardly any reference to national culture according to House et al. (2004). This book, therefore, aims at filling a desperately unmet need. Yet, its findings could very well apply to leadership in other parts of the world, and particularly in multicultural settings.

The research approach

The approach used in our field research is both eclectic and empirical. It is eclectic because we have made no attempt to develop a comprehensive conceptual model or theory. Instead, various perspectives were used to facilitate an investigation of how successful leaders are made, and how they behave as outstanding leaders. Earlier international research findings on leadership, including our own, are incorporated throughout this study.

The approach is also empirical. The data were collected through semi-structured interviews with 310 leaders from 129 organizations in 12 countries: six Gulf Cooperation Council (GCC) countries, and six Northern Arab countries. The leaders were selected from various types of industries, ownerships, and sizes. We made sure to interview leaders from family firms whose founders have passed the management reigns to their children or to professional managers, and we included in our sample some entrepreneurs who are still managing their own companies. Appendix A describes the research methodology and shows some of the relevant statistical analyses.

The lengthy interviews (averaging over one hour) were conducted in confidence by a team of ten experienced Meirc consultants, whose dedication, time, and efforts are recognized in the Acknowledgments. The interviewing process started in mid May 2009 and was completed ten months later in March 2010. In a subsequent follow-up study, 45 additional Lebanese executives were interviewed thus making a total of 76 Lebanese leaders, all of whom are now living and working in three places: Lebanon, GCC countries, and the US. The findings of this subsequent study are presented in Appendix C.

Incidentally, although the interviews were conducted in English, a large number of them were conducted in a mix of English and Arabic, since interviewees and interviewers were fluent in both languages. (The 18 competencies used in the questionnaire were translated to

Arabic, and were placed next to the original English version). The questionnaire can be found in Appendix B.

Main contributions to leadership studies

Our four primary contributions to the field of leadership are presented in Chapters 1, 2, and 3, and Appendix C. *The first contribution*, Chapter 1, links the three concepts of leadership, followership, and culture. This linkage sets the right landscape for looking at the elephant that is leadership from various perspectives, including a multicultural perspective.

The second contribution appears in Chapter 2, "A Framework for Understanding Leadership Success," where we introduce a new framework that shapes how the current field research was designed and conducted (Figure 2.1). It is a three-level approach to understanding leadership success. First, we went back to the earliest childhood and life experiences of leaders in search of factors, events, and people that had significant impact on our leaders. Then, we moved on to find out which leadership competencies helped leaders become outstanding. Finally, we explored the perennial questions, "What makes some leaders more successful than others?" and "What great leaders must do exceptionally well to succeed."

Rudyard Kipling's famous verse that appears at the beginning of this Introduction inspired the "Framework." As mentioned earlier, we asked "when, where, and how" leaders acquire the basic ingredients for success, then we inquired into "what" leadership competencies and styles are essential for success, and "who" succeeded more than others and finally, "why" did they do so. To complete this task, we took into account many scholarly sources, among them the research by Bennis (1989, 2009) on leadership, Muna (1980) on Arab executives, Meirc Training & Consulting (1989) on the ingredients for managerial success, and Hofstede (2001) on culture. We then examined the writings of Goleman (Goleman, Boyatzis, and McKee, 2002) on emotional intelligence (EI) and leadership success, and finally we considered the main points made by de Bono (1985) and Gladwell (2008) about success. The framework provides a useful context for a broader and better understanding of leadership.

The third contribution is our integration and synthesis of the current thinking on the subject of leadership, which, supported by our research data, ultimately revealed a number of paths to leadership success. In Chapter 3, "A Road Map to Success," we discuss the factors that influenced the careers of the outstanding leaders whom we interviewed, namely, what ingredients were necessary for their success. It also explores possible paths that potential leaders can follow on their leadership journey. We present a road map (a diagram) that synthesizes a great amount of significant leadership literature, and also incorporates and integrates the current research. The "Paths to Leadership Success" diagram (Figure 3.1) becomes a template where we weave in our research data and findings. The diagram is made up of three interrelated developmental stages:

- The early years of potential leaders (the basic and early ingredients for success),
- The making of outstanding leaders (learning to become an outstanding leader), and
- The styles and focal action areas of outstanding leaders (what leaders must do exceptionally well to become successful).

Our fourth contribution is to confirm that context, situation, and culture do matter in leadership studies, as demonstrated throughout the book. In Appendix C, we present a study of three groups of Lebanese executives, all born and raised in Lebanon, but who are working in three different parts of the world: Lebanon, GCC countries, and the US. Their leadership styles and decision-making styles differed significantly in the three parts of the world. These Lebanese executives adapted their styles and behavior to the new contexts and cultures in order to be more successful when leading followers from diverse or different cultures.

In Chapter 4, "The Early Years of Potential Leaders," we start presenting our field research findings. First we show how the outstanding leaders were identified and give examples of their accomplishments. Then we move to explore the early years of potential leaders, the role of the ingredients of success, the people and events and how these eventually influenced the careers of the leaders we interviewed.

Chapter 5, "Paths to Outstanding Leadership," is devoted to four of the five paths that potential leaders need to follow in order to become truly outstanding. We will also discuss at length the topic of cultural sensitivity—a critical skill that is essential for leaders who work for or with multinational organizations, and for expatriates, especially in today's and tomorrow's global economy.

Chapter 6, "Learning to Lead: Cultivating Emotional Intelligence," covers the fifth path: emotional intelligence competencies that contributed to the success of Middle Eastern leaders. The research data related to emotional intelligence will be weaved in and compared with international research on the same topic.

"Styles of Emotionally Intelligent Leaders," Chapter 7, presents our research findings on the leadership styles of Middle Eastern leaders as they relate to emotional intelligence. Comparisons with other international research findings on this subject are also presented.

In Chapter 8, we present the decision-making styles of the leaders we interviewed, and we compare the results with the earlier studies by Muna (1980) and Meirc (1989), pointing out the major changes that took place over the last 30 years. The interrelated concepts of execution and performance accountability will also be explored.

Chapter 9, "Recruiting and Developing Talent," highlights the importance of recruiting, retaining, and developing future leaders. These vital tasks were recurring themes throughout most of the interviews with the leaders who participated in our research. Two themes are highlighted. First, great CEOs do not delegate or abdicate the task of developing talent. Second, developing leaders with multicultural and worldly perspectives will become a crucial task in the twenty-first century.

Finally, Chapter 10, "Final Thoughts," concludes with our reflections and recommendations on the subject of leadership success, with special emphasis on the people whose actions, or lack thereof, can impact leadership development in the future. We end with specific recommendations for future research.

In brief, *Developing Multicultural Leaders* will be particularly valuable to current and aspiring leaders from any part of the world. It should be of great interest to CEOs, senior executives, and human resources professionals wishing to cultivate an environment conducive to leadership development within their organizations. It will be also helpful for expatriates working in the Middle East and to multinational organizations doing business there.

Part I

Looking at the Whole Elephant

1

On Leadership, Followership, and Culture

> *It struck me long ago that we make an exaggerated distinction between leaders and followers. The ability to attract and inspire followers is part of the very definition of leadership, and leaders without followers quickly fade away, however exciting their vision.*
>
> —*Warren Bennis*

On leadership

The very concept of leadership is amorphous and elusive. It is hard to define in a manner that is satisfactory to everyone. There is, however, consensus among academics and practitioners that leadership is highly situational and contextual: the leader who succeeds in one context at one point in time will not necessarily succeed in a different context at the same time, or in the same context at a different time, or in different cultures, or even with a different group of followers. Moreover, most writers agree that leadership can be taught and learned, even though others believe that certain leadership talents are inborn. This is an ongoing debate that we shall certainly address.

In this book, *Developing Multicultural Leaders*, the term leadership is used generically and is not necessarily restricted to those at the top of large organizations. It refers to both people who are appointed or selected to be in charge of organizations or institutions (the capital *L*'s), as well as to those who find themselves leading smaller groups, teams, units, or departments within organizations (the small *l*'s). We would like to stress that organizations (and nations for that matter) require both capital *L*'s and small *l*'s. It is equally important to have group leaders scattered at *every* level in the organization. This is not to imply that we should have our organizations populated only by capital *L*'s and small *l*'s: this would be catastrophic (too many chiefs and not enough workers!).

Of course, in addition to leaders (both capital *L's* and small *l's*) we need managers. To fully appreciate this last statement, we borrow from Bennis and Nanus (1985) whose book cover contained these insightful words, "Managers do things right. Leaders do the right thing." This is worth thinking about: managers are efficient, while leaders are effective. Preferably, a balance of leaders and managers should be sought. Ideally, some of those leaders might also be good managers, and some of the managers might be good leaders, as we have found in our research.

On followership and leadership

Like most leaders around the world, the leaders we interviewed for this book were wearing two hats at once: a leadership hat and a follower's hat. Only a few of them did not have bosses—these were the entrepreneurs who still owned the organizations they founded, or the CEOs reporting to boards of directors. But even those few who were not reporting to a superior had many other roles in life in which they were not necessarily leaders, but were most likely followers: they go home every day to their family and spouses, to their neighborhoods, to their community. They belong to social and business associations and clubs where they may very well be followers—not leaders. The popular jest, "The real boss is at home", may be truer than we think!

What are the implications of this? We believe that leadership/followership is a contextual, cultural and, most important, a temporary, time-bound phenomenon. Presidents of countries and CEOs of organizations eventually retire or are replaced, transformed instantly into regular, albeit revered, citizens. Let us take two examples from the American scene, although other countries could serve as good examples too. We have recently witnessed the transition of power after the presidential elections in the US watching how within an hour a new president became the leader of a nation and the outgoing president becomes a "plain" citizen. It is simply a remarkable event to watch, especially for those who live and work in non-democratic countries. Or, consider how the powerful "CEO of the twentieth century," Jack Welch of GE, retired gracefully and became a speaker, magazine columnist, and writer of books. He, too, was a leader and a follower for many years during his career.

But this phenomenon of being at once a leader and a follower is not new; it has been happening since our childhood. As we were growing up, most of us played the role of both leader and follower at home, perhaps with siblings or relatives our age; we may have done the same thing in the neighborhood, or at school, or in university, and most certainly at work. We would venture to say that all of us have had this experience at least several times during our life.

The implications are clear: first, people begin learning leadership at a very young age. Some become outstanding, others never excel at it. Life experiences do matter (both the traumatic and wonderful events), but being at once a leader and follower, we suspect, has the greatest influence on future leadership success. In addition, as confirmed by the current research findings, the shaping of leadership is also greatly influenced by parents or relatives, friends, role models, extracurricular activities during the educational years, early responsibility, reading and self-development, and finally what happens to us after we start a career.

The second implication is that leadership behavior and styles are probably influenced by the expectations and values of followers: a democratic leader could be perceived as a weak leader in some non-democratic cultures. People in certain cultures may prefer being followers, not always for the same reasons suggested by Western literature. The power and hierarchal structures in some societies, for example, may well discourage certain people from seeking leadership roles. Other dimensions of culture may have significant effects on both leadership and followership. We simply do not know for certain what cultural factors influence the dynamic relationship between these two concepts; which brings us to the next implication.

In sum, leadership and followership (and we will add culture) cannot each be examined in isolation. James MacGregor Burns (1978) said it well many years ago when he wrote in his seminal book, *Leadership*:

> One-man leadership is contradiction in terms. Leaders, in responding to their own motives, appeal to the motives of potential

followers. As followers respond, a symbiotic relationship develops that binds leader and follower together.

On culture

A third implication of the above phenomenon is the increasingly urgent and crucial challenge of studying followership, as has been repeatedly stated by Kelley (1988, 2008), O'Toole (1995), Bennis (2009) and other leading scholars. Leadership, however, cannot be understood without understanding its contexts, including the understanding of followership and the national culture of followers. Therefore, future leadership research should be truly multinational and multicultural—not simply exploring and testing Western theories and hypotheses, as has mostly been done so far (including to some extent our own current research). The tides of globalization ebb and flow and, despite the digital information revolution, we cannot be certain if the world is moving toward convergence, at least not in the near future. History tells us that national culture differences are not likely to go away soon.

If followers from different cultures have diverse and distinct backgrounds, beliefs, values, expectations, aspirations, and motivation—a different mindset, then leadership studies must take into consideration these differences. Followership and leadership will undoubtedly be influenced by the cultural backgrounds of both leaders and followers: it is one additional and important variable that cannot be ignored. Our current study of leadership will to some extent reflect such cultural influences, especially their impact on leadership and decision-making styles.

Again, if leaders and followers are indeed influenced by their macro-level societal norms and systems (including family upbringing and schooling), then the cultural impact of these experiences should also be taken into account since societal values and school experiences do differ from one culture to another—and sometimes even within the same country or region. A monumental research carried out by Hofstede (2001) has indicated that management and leadership styles do differ across cultures. His work was later replicated, extended, and confirmed in 62 countries over a period of ten years by a multicultural team of 160 social scientists (House et al., 2004). Once again, however, these studies were meant to replicate and test a European conception of culture's dimensions.

A recent book edited by Nakata (2009) has raised some questions about Hofstede's conceptualization of culture. The contributing writers are scholars from diverse backgrounds and disciplines and come from several continents and cultures (e.g. Danish, Turkish, Chinese, Russian, Canadian, Japanese, American, British). Although they highly praise the work of Hofstede, they call for a different, more dynamic, approach to understanding cultures. They believe that the relationships between national cultures are changing due to increasing interdependence created by globalization, such as interlocking financial and banking systems, and involvement of more people in international trade through partnership and alliances. This is a long-awaited development and is a good start to multicultural understanding of leadership and management. The editor, Nakata, states: "However, because few alternative views have been investigated, the journey has in fact just begun."

On the other hand, Ghemawat (2007) argues convincingly that globalization is not likely to take hold as conventional wisdom has it. Instead, he argues that differences between countries are larger than generally acknowledged, and that "semiglobalization is, in fact, the real state of the world today—and tomorrow." Ghemawat advances a framework that highlights the distances between countries on four components: cultural, administrative, geographic, and economic distances to explain our "semiglobalized" world. Business strategies, he writes, should take advantage of both similarities and differences between countries, and that a one-size-fits-all approach will simply not work.

After a thorough and critical review of the recent research on cross-cultural leadership, Jackson and Parry (2008) conclude: "The growing interest in leadership research throughout the rest of the world has revealed contributions as well as limitations in the applicability and relevance of the predominantly American-based research to other national and local contexts." They add: "Others have argued that it is not just the specificity of the cultures being explored but the culturally specific ways in which they have been explored that has limited our ability to understand the full range and depth of leadership practices throughout the world."

Meanwhile, the research on globalization and its effects on culture, leadership, and followership will, we hope, continue in more earnest—by multicultural teams of scholars. In this book we will examine how national cultures, regional cultures, and multicultural environments influence leadership and decision-making styles in the Middle East.

On success

No book on leadership success would be complete without defining success. It is, after all, the fifth and last word in this book's subtitle! Like leadership, success is an amorphous and elusive term. How do you measure it? Which standards, and whose standards do you apply? Does leadership success imply success only at work? These are good questions that scholars are starting to address when discussing leadership. The following two publications, among many others, attempt to deal with this concept. First, Nash and Stevenson (2004) wrote *Just Enough: Tools for Creating Success in Your Work and Life* where they define success by four categories: Happiness (self), Achievement (work), Significance (family), and Legacy (community). They call for a balance in these categories by presenting a step-by-step "Kaleidoscope Strategy" for addressing each of these components of enduring success in a way that does not shortchange the others. This is how they define each component of success:

Happiness: Feelings of pleasure or contentment about your life;

Achievement: Accomplishments that compare favorably against similar goals others have strived for;

Significance: The sense that you have made a positive impact on people you care about; and

Legacy: A way to establish your values or accomplishments so as to help others find future success.

As we shall see later on, in our current research we have focused on "work achievements" as the criteria for success. In fact, the first open-ended questions that we asked those whom we interviewed were about work accomplishments that were achieved during the last three to four years, and we probed to make certain that these accomplishments were indeed carried out by the interviewees, and what exact role the respondents had in these achievements.

The other publication is an article by Muna and Mansour (2009) titled "Balancing Work and Personal Life: The Leader as Acrobat."

The authors exhort leaders, organizations, and HR professionals to introduce changes in the work environment that encourage a better balance between work and personal life (which includes family, friends, self, and community). They end the article with these words:

> Over the years we have spoken with many senior executives who are nearing or are in retirement. To this day, we have yet to find a single executive who wished that he or she had spent more time at work. On the contrary, the most common thread was their regret of sacrificing their family, friends, and health in favor of dedicating a significantly disproportionate amount of effort and time to demanding work responsibilities.

While we appreciate that working hard, not to forget working smart, is one of the paths to leadership success, we strongly believe that an important ingredient to success would be leading a balanced and "integrated life that augments work with family, friends, community service, spiritual activities, physical exercise, and whatever else matters in one's life" (George and Sims, 2007).

2
A Framework for Understanding Leadership Success

> *The most dangerous leadership myth is that leaders are born—that there is a genetic factor to leadership. This myth asserts that people simply either have certain charismatic qualities or not. That's nonsense; in fact, the opposite is true. Leaders are made rather than born.*
>
> *—Warren Bennis*

> *If you wish to plan for a year, sow seeds,*
> *If you wish to plan for ten years, plant trees,*
> *If you wish to plan for a lifetime, develop people.*
> *—Kuan Chung Tzu (Seventh century BC)*

> *Chance favors the prepared mind.*
>
> *—Louis Pasteur*

What are the secrets of leadership success? What makes some leaders more successful than others? To help us answer these perennial questions, this chapter offers a new framework for understanding leadership success by looking at leadership from three different perspectives.

The subject of leadership has been discussed in many cultures for thousands of years. To say that there is a plethora of literature on leadership would be a great understatement; there are thousands and thousands of articles, books, videos, and CDs on leadership. Indeed, there has been no dearth of resources on leadership, especially in the last four decades. Some—a very few—are, however, worth exploring and we shall refer to those as and when needed.

Many scholars and practitioners have attempted to explain the concept of leadership and the secrets of successful leaders from very specific and sometimes narrow perspectives. For instance, the attempt to investigate the traits of successful leaders was inconclusive, and researchers could not arrive at a definitive list of attributes. Another attempt examined leadership styles to determine which styles work best in different situations. A third approach looked at competencies used by successful leaders at different levels. A more recent approach explored emotional intelligence and talent.

Note that each of these approaches has contributed incrementally to our understanding of leadership. We believe that all are necessary and helpful to develop leadership effectiveness, and that they are interrelated. But each of these efforts was analogous to viewing the "proverbial elephant" from different angles and perspectives. We desperately need to integrate these approaches into a new framework that allows us to form a more accurate picture of the "whole elephant." We need to uncover the mystique that shrouds the enigmatic concept of leadership. Therefore, to put things in a better and wider perspective, we will explore this subject using Rudyard Kipling's famous verse:

> I keep six honest serving-men
> (They taught me all I knew);
> Their names were What and Why and When
> And How and Where and Who.

When, where, and how leadership starts?

"When, where and how" do people acquire the necessary competencies that lead to success? Here, we will be probing for answers to the following questions: Are some of the leadership characteristics genetic and some learned? Are they acquired during childhood or adulthood? Are they learned through experience, and if so, what type of experience? Are they acquired through management and leadership training? In short, what are the *sources* of the ingredients that lead to success?

Our earlier research (Muna, 1980; Meirc, 1989; Muna, 2003), conducted through extensive open-ended interviews with hundreds of executives, showed that there are ten "ingredients for success" which seem to have given organizational leaders a considerable edge. It is worth emphasizing that the top five of these ten "ingredients" are acquired during childhood and the educational years, well before a person enters the workforce. It is also worth mentioning at this time that hardly any of the leaders had all five of these ingredients.

Charles Handy, an international management thinker, described the findings of the 1989 Meirc study in his book *Beyond Certainty* in a chapter titled "Teach Your Children Well" using these words:

> I was recently given the unusual opportunity to be adviser to a study of the education and development of Arab executives (*The Making of Gulf Managers: A Study of Successful Managers in the GCC Countries*, by Dr. Farid Muna for Meirc). I know little if anything about Arab executives, so it seemed sensible to start by asking some of the best of them how they had been helped to get as far as they had in life, and what hindered them. Nearly 200 executives were identified by over 50 organizations as notably successful and those were each interviewed at length and in confidence.
>
> The results were fascinating, partly because what they said is almost certainly true of successful executives in any other culture, including our own.
>
> (Handy, 1996)

In Chapter 4, we shall discover whether these ten ingredients are still valid for the leaders recently interviewed in 12 countries. Meanwhile, here is a brief description of the top five ingredients:

- **Quality of education**: With emphasis on the acquisition of both analytical and creative thinking skills rather than rote learning and high grades. Learning social and emotional skills through extracurricular activities (sports, student clubs, drama, music, arts and so on) during kindergarten, school, and university years.
- **Early responsibility**: Through discipline, small tasks and assignments given by parents and first managers, or simply prompted by the economic need to earn money while still in school. Early responsibilities will allow people to assume greater responsibilities in their future career and will certainly make younger people appreciate the value of money.

- **Ethics and values**: Importance of integrity and commitment, hard work, quality, and respect for the value of time—all of which are greatly influenced by child upbringing and culture, especially so in the case of some immigrants and minorities.
- **Self development**: An insatiable thirst and passion for continuous learning and self-improvement throughout life: always having an active inquiring mind. This is instilled in people early on by parents, teachers, peers, and other role models.
- **Exposure and role models**: Provided through parents' influence, travel, working or socializing with foreigners, learning from others, and learning from the school of life. Role models are those who have exerted great positive influence on us; they are the people whom we admire, respect, and aspire to emulate or to please. Role models are those people who keep encouraging us to excel, sometimes long after they are gone.

The importance of these ingredients is clearly seen when one observes (a) admission procedures at top universities and (b) recruitment of new graduates for future leadership positions. Of course, good grades and high scores on scholastic tests are important for admission to excellent universities, but more and more of the top universities are also looking closely at the student's extracurricular accomplishments for admission decisions. Universities are likely to ask if a student was actively engaged in sports, drama, arts, student clubs, and whether he or she did any part-time, summer, or community work. Such students would have had the rich experience of interacting with high caliber students and teachers, stretching of the mind, and learning to socialize and be part of a team.

Similarly, excellent companies will give equal, if not more, weight to analytical thinking and interpersonal skills as compared to high grades when recruiting university graduates. Ask yourself this question (which we ask executives attending our management seminars): "Which of these two candidates would you hire for a future leadership job: the first graduate with outstanding grades, say, with a Grade Point Average (GPA) of 3.9 out of 4.0, who spent most of his or her time going from home to class to the library, or the second graduate with a 3.0 average who was active in sports, student associations, and who earned some of the tuition fees by working during school semesters and during summer breaks?" Invariably, most executives would choose the second student, especially if both candidates graduated from the same university with the same major. The second graduate would have had many opportunities to learn the importance of teamwork, leadership, followership, communication and social skills. He or she would also have benefited greatly from the "early responsibility" of working hard during university years.

Similar ingredients were cited over the years by several writers. For example, the classic book on leadership *On Becoming a Leader* by Warren Bennis (1989), and the more recent *True North* by Bill George and Peter Sims (2007) have emphasized life experiences as one of the main ingredients of success.

Bennis wrote: "I would argue that more leaders have been made by accident, circumstance, sheer grit, or will than have been made by all the leadership courses put together. Leadership courses can only teach skills. Developing character and vision is the way leaders invent themselves." He asserts that to become a true leader, one must know the world (context) as well as know one's self. According to Bennis, studies demonstrate that certain kinds of experiences are especially significant for learning. "These experiences include broad and continuing education, idiosyncratic families, extensive travel and/or exile, a rich private life, and key associations with mentors and groups."

In a short commentary which appeared in Bennis' recent book, *The Essential Bennis*, Bill George summarized a central point of his book in these words:

> Among the 125 successful and authentic leaders interviewed for my book, *True North*, none suggested that their traits, characteristics, or competencies led to their success. Instead, most said that their life stories and experiences provided the passion, purpose, and values by which they lead. Over three-quarters identified a specific transformative experience, which Bennis terms a crucible, as the most important factor in their success. It was through the crucible—or through reframing it years later—that they discovered the authentic leadership that enabled them to become fully integrated leaders.
>
> (Bennis, 2009)

In the book *True North* the authors went into more detail; they wrote: "The stories of authentic leaders cover the full spectrum of life's experiences. They include the impact of parents, teachers, coaches, and mentors who recognized their potential; the impact of their communities; and their leadership in team sports, scouting, student government, and early employment."

Thinking and acting strategically has been a significant attribute of successful leaders, according to many scholars and practitioners. Again, we find that strategic thinking is acquired over several years; through various early life experiences, and nourished by a supportive organizational climate which encourages initiative, creativity, and calculated risk taking. For instance, in her book, *Learning to Think Strategically*, Sloan (2006) argued that it is a myth that only a few people can learn strategic thinking—it is not an inborn talent, but one that can be learned and cultivated. Sloan highlights the importance of informal learning, prior successful life experiences, dialogue, and the coordination between intuition and analytical thinking.

Similarly, Goldman (2007) found that "expertise in strategic thinking is not the product of innate ability and pure serendipity. It arises from specific experiences (personal, interpersonal, organizational and external) which occur over ten years or more." Goldman's research revealed ten experiences that contributed to the development of strategic thinking: family upbringing/education; general work experiences; becoming a CEO; being mentored; being challenged by a key colleague; monitoring results/benchmarking; doing strategic planning; spearheading a major growth initiative; dealing with a threat to organizational survival; and vicarious experiences.

In short, early life experiences at home, the quality of learning and extracurricular activities at school and university, early work responsibilities, role models and mentors—all seem to have profound impact on developing character and vision of a leader. The implications of these findings are enormous when it comes to child upbringing, education, and recruitment—a topic that we shall return to later in the book.

What are the necessary competencies for leadership success?

Next, we will focus on "what" great leaders do and how they behave in order to become successful. Included in the "what" rubric of leadership are the characteristics, styles, competencies, and the key areas of action that leaders focus on.

Recent thinking has focused on the subjects of competencies, emotional intelligence, and talent. For example, Boyatzis explored managerial competencies many years ago when he wrote *The Competent Manager* (1982); he was building on the seminal work of the late David McClelland (1973), a noted Harvard University psychologist. More recently, Daniel Goleman who has been writing on emotional intelligence since 1995 reemphasized McClelland's thesis by stating that emotional intelligence (EI) is equally, if not more, essential for success than cognitive abilities, commonly measured by Intelligence Quotient (IQ) tests. Although the current EI model has been criticized by some social scientists for its lack of predictive power, the arguments put forth by proponents of EI make a lot of intuitive sense: high IQ scores do not necessarily translate into success in business or in social relations; feelings and emotional competencies surely have a great influence on leadership success.

In their book *Primal Leadership: Realizing the Power of Emotional Intelligence* (2002), Goleman, Boyatzis, and McKee listed the following 18 EI competencies under four categories:

- **Self-awareness**: Accurate self-assessment, self-confidence, and emotional self-awareness.
- **Self-management**: Emotional self-control, transparency, adaptability, initiative, optimism, and achievement.
- **Social awareness**: Empathy, organizational awareness, and service orientation.
- **Relationship management**: Inspirational leadership, change catalyst, teamwork and collaboration, developing others, influence, and managing conflict.

Most of these competencies are related to success not only in leadership but in other social situations. Primal leadership, according to the authors, refers to the emotional dimension of leadership, where a leader's primal task is to articulate a message or a vision that resonates with their followers—this primal task is an emotional task.

There is little doubt that social scientists will continue to debate the efficacy of EI competencies in predicting success. Nevertheless, a high IQ score (how high no one knows for sure) does not by itself guarantee leadership success.

Who succeeds, and why some succeed more than others?

What about Kipling's remaining friends, "why and who"? Here, we will ask "who" succeeds and "why" some leaders achieved great success while others did not.

Edward de Bono (1985), known for his concept of lateral thinking, wrote in his book *Tactics: The Art and Science of Success* that success depends on any of these four factors:

- **Luck**: de Bono states that a person with a positive attitude toward luck "is able to carry to success whatever turns up by luck ... this attitude means that you are very ready to spot opportunities, and it also means that you may generate such opportunities deliberately."
- **Determination**: as indicated by single-mindedness, persistence and a strong sense of direction. Edward de Bono calls this type of determination "a little madness." He adds: "You may have these qualities by temperament or as a strategy."
- **Talent**: Whether natural or acquired through training, talent seems to be an important ingredient to most success. He adds: "Where there seems to be no natural talent, then it makes sense to substitute for talent by hard work, training, experience, and strategy."
- **The right place and situation**: de Bono uses the term "rapid growth field" to describe places and situations in which it is much easier to be successful than in others. His advice is to "try to choose not only an opportunity field but preferably a growing one."

The book by Malcolm Gladwell (2008), *Outliers: The Story of Success*, though written for the general public in a journalistic rather than scientific or academic manner, puts forward similar ideas about success. It is a pity that Gladwell does not expound on, or even refer to, the growing body of literature on EI.

Gladwell asserts that success is related not only to IQ but to other variables, such as:

- The **luck** of being born in a certain era (or even month) that gives people a greater competitive advantage. He cites the age-advantage of Canadian hockey players born in the first quarter of a year; persons who came of age when the PC became widely available; and those lawyers and entrepreneurs (children of poor immigrants) who were at the right age and place when deregulation of the financial markets took place.

- **Preparedness and hard work:** Gladwell refers to "The 10,000-hour rule" of work and practice which gave many people the edge. He provides examples of Bill Joy's contributions to UNIX, Java; and the Internet; Mozart's masterwork when he was 21; the Beatles and their Hamburg experience of playing music eight hours a day, seven days a week between 1960 and 1962; and Bill Gates who put in thousands of hours of computer programming starting at the age of 13.

- **Influence of parents and culture:** Gladwell cites the influence of parents, and especially migrant parents, who instill hard work and ambition in their children. He also cites the example of Chinese culture when it comes to the hard and back-breaking work of cultivating rice (it is unfortunate that Gladwell does not mention the effect of the Protestant work ethics which contributed to Capitalism and the Industrial Revolution).

- **Education:** Gladwell attributes more school days per year and longer hours to better scholastic achievements, even among poorer communities. Examples are given from New York's KIPP Academy public schools, and the longer school year in some countries (220 school days in South Korea and 243 days in Japan, as compared to 180 days in the US).

De Bono's and Gladwell's writings echo the research carried out by Meirc in 1989 and by Muna in 2003, and verify the argument that IQ alone is not sufficient to explain success. Thus, it appears that what matters most is not IQ alone, nor the quality of education, child upbringing, culture and work ethics by themselves, nor EI competencies in isolation. It appears that opportunity, luck and personal circumstances may also partially explain the success of some people. In fact, it is a combination of all these factors that contributes to leadership success.

A framework for understanding leadership success

We believe that it is time to share with our readers an overall framework (Figure 2.1) integrating and making sense of all three

Who? Why?	Opportunity, determination and hard work, luck, and cultural circumstances
What?	Competencies (skills, knowledge, and EI)
When? Where? How?	Child upbringing, early responsibility, quality of education, self-development, role models, and work ethics

Figure 2.1 A framework for understanding leadership success

approaches. Kipling's six honest serving-men, shown on the left, have helped us to see more clearly the "whole elephant" that is leadership.

Does this mean that *all* of the above elements (shown on the right) are prerequisites for success? *Of course not!* In our study of the ingredients for success it was found that not all ingredients were present for every manager, but it was clear that the more ingredients a person possesses or exhibits, the greater are his or her chances of becoming successful. Similarly, it is unlikely that leaders have mastery in all 18 EI competencies identified by Goleman. And it is also unlikely that successful people would get breaks in all the areas identified by de Bono and Gladwell. Clearly, leaders with fewer numbers of ingredients or with competencies that need improvement can overcome such shortcomings through proper training and development, if they are motivated to do so. And, let us always keep in mind Louis Pasteur's astute observation that "Chance favors the prepared mind."

Although the above discussion is based mostly on a combination of scientific research, conventional wisdom, and personal observations, the implications for educational reform, child upbringing, leadership development and training, and recruitment are immense. Identifying the key elements underlying leadership success remains a critical subject and one worthy of continuing research. Undoubtedly, a better understanding of leadership will have significant implications for organizations: more effective recruitment, development, and retention of future leaders will eventually be reflected in better overall organizational performance.

Accordingly, we at Meirc Training & Consulting launched this research study covering one of the important regions of the world, the Middle East, in order to add a multicultural perspective to the ongoing leadership debate. The research will also answer the questions posed at the beginning of this chapter: "What makes some leaders more successful than others?" "What are the secrets for leadership success?" "What paths can potential leaders take on their journey to leadership success?" Using this new framework allows us to look at the entire "elephant" from several angles and perspectives.

3
A Road Map to Success

*Leadership is autobiographical: if I don't know your life
story, I don't know a thing about you as a leader.*

—Noel Tichy

*Leaders aren't born—at least not full blown. Neither
are they made like instant coffee. Instead they are slow
brewed.*

—Joseph and Jimmie Boyett

How many paths are there to leadership success? Are there any
common ingredients that lead to success? And if so, what messages
are there for developing future managers and leaders? This chapter
provides answers to these important questions.

In this chapter, we will present a road map (or a diagram) that
synthesizes a great amount of significant leadership literature
and incorporates and integrates our current research, using a
multicultural perspective. The diagram is made up of three interrelated parts: the early years; the paths that lead to leadership
success; and the styles and action areas which great leaders must
excel at.

The "Paths to Leadership Success" road map

Even though there is a small number of management "gurus"
who think that leadership is mainly genetic or charismatic, our
findings indicate that leadership is learned throughout life.

In fact, we have discovered that the paths to leadership success are varied and multifaceted. Typically, some leaders are born with certain genetic attributes (IQ and stamina, for example), then they learn from their parents, teachers, peer groups, and from early life experiences, including personal traumas and crises. They are also influenced by the cultural norms, values, and social systems of their cultures.

Later, leaders acquire and cultivate the necessary leadership and technical skills through challenging work experiences (learning from both success and failure), and by direct or indirect mentoring and coaching from their own managers and colleagues. They acquire their knowledge and skills by reading avidly, and by attending courses, seminars and conferences. Leaders are always prepared to seek and grab the opportunities that luck or circumstances bring their way. Finally, outstanding leaders are determined, persistent, and work really hard to achieve their aims.

In brief, learning to become a great leader is a lifelong process if one has the desire, motivation and the thirst for continuous self-development. Learning to lead is a journey with several paths along the way.

In an effort to integrate and synthesize our own research findings with some of the theories and studies of earlier scholars and practitioners, we created a visual diagram that we called Paths to leadership success (see Figure 3.1). The diagram depicts the relationships between the early ingredients for success (the early years), five paths to success (the making of outstanding leaders), and the styles and key focus or action areas in which outstanding leaders must do exceptionally well.

The group of outstanding leaders we interviewed, collectively, revealed that some or most of these five paths were valuable to them during their leadership journey. These paths, we believe, are also the most frequently mentioned in the leadership literature. We certainly realize that there may be other paths, but we will focus on those five that were most frequently mentioned by the leaders we interviewed for this book.

In brief, a potential leader can learn to become an outstanding one if he or she has the opportunity to follow some of these paths. Of course, we will not attempt to discuss in depth all the topics shown under the three headings at the top of Figure 3.1—that would simply

The early years of potential leaders (Chapter 3)	The making of outstanding leaders (Chapters 4 and 5)	What outstanding leaders do exceptionally well (Chapters 6, 7 and 8)
Early life experiences and quality of education	Cultivating EI competencies	Motivational leadership styles
Upbringing, work ethics and values	Working hard and smart	Decision-making and performance accountability
	Training and career development	Recruiting and developing talent
Genes and cultural factors	Personal development	
	Cultural sensitivity	Vision, strategy and execution

Figure 3.1   **Paths to leadership success**

not do justice to the existing leadership literature. Instead, we will weave in our research findings when and where appropriate in the next six chapters.

The early years of potential leaders (the basic and early ingredients for success)

Let us summarize the factors that appear on the left side of Figure 3.1. The reader will notice that we have introduced the term *potential leader* in the diagram. Research findings, including ours, have shown that all or most of the factors on the left side of the diagram are crucial in preparing people for future leadership positions. As mentioned earlier, our research shows that it is unlikely (and unnecessary) that potential leaders would experience all the early ingredients for success. Moreover, research also shows that these occur well before a person starts a career. In other words, potential leaders have experienced some of these three factors, namely:

First, their early life experiences (both happy and sad events), together with the quality of their educational experience were repeatedly mentioned by the managers and leaders we interviewed as having profound influences on their thinking and ultimately their future behavior. In Chapter 4, we will list some examples of events and people that had an impact on potential leaders.

Second, the leaders' upbringing and especially the work ethics and values inculcated in them at a young age had a tremendous impact on their personal values, integrity, and character. Nearly all the leaders we interviewed mentioned one or more role models who had a powerful impact on their careers. The most frequently mentioned role models (boss, father, teacher, and so on) are analyzed in Chapter 4.

Third, some of our respondents believed that certain characteristics were genetic (IQ and stamina, for example); and this remains a controversial topic. Additionally, crises and traumatic events, as well as cultural factors (such as religious beliefs, family and social pressures, and cultural beliefs and norms) have played a significant role in the formation of the personalities and value systems of potential leaders.

The making of outstanding leaders (learning to become a great leader)

Past and current research findings indicate that for potential leaders to become *outstanding leaders*, they must at sometime in their careers follow some, if not most, of the paths outlined in the middle of the diagram. While the paths are listed sequentially, they may occur concurrently in real life. For example, a leader can be cultivating his or her competencies while at the same time gaining technical knowledge and managerial experience. Another leader may be working hard, and at the same time reading avidly and learning from his or her mentors or role models, and so on.

As we shall see in Chapter 5, most of the outstanding leaders told us that their success was mainly due to taking some or most of the five paths shown in Figure 3.1: they cultivated their emotional intelligence; they worked hard and smart; they were exposed to training or career development activities, and learned from these exposures; and they developed themselves by reading avidly and learning from the experience of others as well as their own. Many of them commented on how they learned from other nationalities: from expatriates working in their countries; or from exposure to overseas assignments; or by working in multinational organizations. On the other hand, the frequency of mention and the impact of these five paths were much less with the excellent and successful managers. In sum, outstanding managers became outstanding because they took some, if not all, the paths shown in Figure 3.1.

Incidentally, we have included a competency that is not often found in the leadership literature, namely, cultural sensitivity. Learning from exposure to different nationalities and cultures, and hence the ability to bridge cultures, was mentioned often by the outstanding leaders we interviewed. Cultural sensitivity is a competency that we believe is particularly critical for those who work for or with multinational organizations or in multicultural settings.

Chapters 5 and 6 are entirely devoted to these five paths.

What outstanding leaders do exceptionally well (what leaders must excel at to succeed)

Finally, great leaders must become keenly aware of the effect that leadership and decision-making styles have on people and organizations. Leaders must also focus their efforts on developing their people's talent in line with a carefully formulated long-term strategy in order to achieve success. Finally, effective leaders must execute their organizational strategies well, and hold themselves and others accountable for their actions. Most of the areas on the right side of Figure 3.1 were indeed mentioned by a large number of our interviewees, and were reconfirmed by our review and synthesis of the literature on leadership. The topics that appear under the heading "What outstanding leaders do exceptionally well" will be discussed in Chapters 7, 8 and 9.

In addition to the writings of the scholars and practitioners that were mentioned earlier, particularly the collection of essays written by Warren Bennis (2009) over the span of more than four decades, we present below examples from the tables of contents of three books that had an influence on our thinking when developing this road map. The reader will notice that most, if not all, of the topics which appear on the right side of Figure 3.1 are also discussed in these earlier works, especially the topic we called "Recruiting and Developing Talent", which is covered by all three books (see subjects highlighted in italics followed by an asterisk).

Collins and Porras, *Built to Last: Successful Habits of Visionary Companies* (1994)

- Big Hairy Audacious Goals
- Cult-Like Culture
- Try Lot of Stuff and Keep What Works
- *Home-Grown Management**
- Good Enough Never Is
- Building the Vision

Joyce, Nohria, and Roberson, *What Really Works: The 4+2 Formula for Sustained Business Success* (2003)

- Make Your Strategy Clear and Focused
- Execute Flawlessly
- Build a Performance-Based Culture
- Make Your Organization Fast and Flat
- *Make Talent Stick Around and Develop More**
- Make Your Leaders Committed to Your Business
- Make Industry-Transforming Innovations
- Make Growth Happen with Mergers and Partnerships

Ulrich, Smallwood, and Sweetman, *The Leadership Code: Five Rules to Lead By* (2008)

- Shape the Future (Strategist)
- Make Things Happen (Executor)
- Engage Today's Talent (Talent Manager)
- *Build the Next Generation (Human Capital Developer)**
- Invest in Yourself (Personal Proficiency)

To put things in a broader perspective, we would like to share with our readers a quote by John Zenger, a leadership expert, which appeared in *The Leadership Code* by Ulrich, Smallwood, and Sweetman (2008); a quote whose words we wholeheartedly agree with and which was supported to a great extent by our own findings.

> I think ... that 85 per cent of the competencies in various competency models appear to be the same. I think that we have a relatively good handle on the necessary competencies for a leader to possess in order to be effective. But there are some other variables that competency models do not account for. [Among] the

variables that I think we don't account for include ... the leader's personal situation (family pressures, economics, competition, social, etc); [and] internal influences, such as health, energy, vitality, resilience, the intensity of effort the individual is willing to put forth, ambition and drive, willingness to sacrifice.

To conclude, there is much more to understanding leadership success than studying competencies, leadership traits, or leadership styles in isolation. And that is precisely why we have examined the three leadership development stages shown in Figure 3.1.

To reiterate, understanding the whole elephant involves looking at:

- First, the events that influenced potential leaders well before they started their careers.
- Second, the paths leaders can choose to follow in order to become outstanding.
- Third, the main areas outstanding leaders must focus on, and must excel at, including using the most effective leadership and decision-making styles.

Figure 3.1 will be our road map for the next six chapters. The journey to leadership success begins now as we end this chapter with a quotation from Henry David Thoreau:

As a single footstep will not make a path on the earth, so a single thought will not make a pathway in the mind. To make a deep physical path, we walk again and again. To make a deep mental path, we must think over and over the kind of thoughts we wish to dominate our lives.

Part II

The Making of Outstanding Leaders

4
The Early Years of Potential Leaders

Give a man a fish, and you feed him for a day;
Teach a man to fish, and you feed him for a lifetime.
—*Chinese proverb*

If your actions inspire others to dream more, learn more,
do more and become more, you are a leader.
—*John Quincy Adams*

In this chapter, we will first explain the criteria that were used to identify leadership success among the leaders we interviewed for this book.
We will discuss the factors that influenced the careers of those leaders
and managers; in other words, what ingredients were necessary for their
success. Examples of their accomplishments will be presented, as well as
examples of the events, people and other factors that influenced them.

We then focus on the early years of potential leaders. Potential
leaders are those people who have had some, not necessarily all, of
the basic ingredients for success well before they start their managerial careers. Potential leaders, we believe, have a number of future
opportunities and paths to follow to become outstanding.

How we identified leadership success

The following is a brief explanation of how we identified the outstanding leaders among the managers we interviewed. Although the managers selected by their organizations were all considered successful
leaders, we went further to find out who among them were more

successful than others. The selection criteria used by the organization was, therefore, the initial screening. To differentiate further, we used two additional methods.

First, we decided at the outset that additional criteria should be used to distinguish between successful and outstanding performance. Using content analysis of the interviews, the accomplishments of each person were coded as *successful, excellent,* or *outstanding.* The Meirc interviewers made the initial coding in accordance with predetermined standards. Many scholars have used this method of categorization in the past.

Meirc interviewers asked respondents probing questions to find out the number and nature of accomplishments over the past three to four years, and whether these accomplishments were indeed originated and carried out by the respondents themselves. For example, we asked: who originated the idea, whether the respondents encountered any difficulties or resistance to their new ideas or systems, what specific role their immediate manager played in these accomplishments, whether it was an individual or team effort, and what role did subordinates play.

Second, these initial codes were subsequently crosschecked and occasionally adjusted by the authors in order to ensure overall consistency and increased reliability. Our standards for the coding were the following:

Successful: involving successfully carrying out the basic job functions or successfully implementing projects/ideas as suggested or initiated by upper management.

Excellent: involving active leadership and participation in significant advances in performance at the individual and group levels (e.g. improvements in productivity or quality of work).

Outstanding: involving multiple, highly innovative, and significant contributions that led to (a) the betterment of national employees; and/or (b) productivity, cost improvement, customer service, or marketing; and/or (c) enhancement of organizational objectives and strategies.

The outstanding leaders

Of the 310 persons we interviewed, 33 percent were considered successful, 38 percent excellent, and 29 percent were outstanding. Table 4.1 shows the results by nationality. Not surprising, the

Table 4.1 Accomplishments by nationality (listed alphabetically)

Nationality	Successful	Excellent	Outstanding	Total
Bahraini	8	4	8	20
Egyptian	7	8	5	20
Iraqi	5	11	5	21
Jordanian	8	9	5	22
Kuwaiti	8	6	6	20
Lebanese	8	14	9	31
Omani	5	10	5	20
Palestinian	8	6	7	21
Qatari	6	9	6	21
Saudi Arabian	18	17	15	50
Syrian	9	7	5	21
Emirati (UAE)	14	16	13	43
Total	104	117	89	310
Percent	33%	38%	29%	100%

Note: In the earlier study covering 140 Gulf managers, the results were: Successful 28 percent, Excellent 48 percent, and Outstanding 24 percent (Meirc Training & Consulting, 1989).

outstanding leaders were found among all 12 nationalities. A chi-square test showed no statistically significant differences among the 12 nationalities (chi-square = 10.43, df = 22). Similarly, there were no statistically significant differences between nationals of the six Gulf Cooperation Council countries (chi-square = 5.08, df = 10) or significant differences between nationals of the six Northern Arab countries (chi-square = 4.50, df = 10).

The outstanding leaders, however, distinguished themselves from the others by their significant, creative, and often audacious contributions. Their work accomplishments are different because of their nature and the number of them that occurred during the past three to four years. The quality and the number of accomplishments of the outstanding leaders were significantly higher than the accomplishments of the other leaders. For example, the average number of principal accomplishments in the last three to four years was 3.4 accomplishments, compared to 2.3 for the excellent leaders, and 1.5 for the successful leaders. However, when coding we looked closely at the magnitude and quality of the achievements, not just the number of them.

We were impressed by the very words used by outstanding leaders to describe these contributions. The outstanding leaders "launched," "initiated," "introduced," "developed," "promoted," "instigated," and "pioneered" new systems, processes, or ideas. They "trained," "coached," and "developed" their people for the long run. They "built" effective teams. In short, their contributions were not only more numerous, but were also more proactive, visionary, bold, and innovative when compared to those cited by the other leaders.

We discovered that the outstanding leaders have certainly taken some of the paths mentioned earlier that led to their success such as working hard and smart, developing themselves, learning from others, and learning from their own work experience, including both successes and failures.

We were not surprised to find that outstanding leaders came from all three levels of management (top, middle, and lower levels). In fact, we invited the organizations to nominate successful leaders from all levels (see the letter of invitation in Appendix B). When looking closer at the data, we found that there were statistically significant differences between levels (and age) and the quantity and quality of accomplishments. The results shown in Table 4.2 reveal the following:

- Forty-four percent (44%) of outstanding leaders from upper management levels were considered outstanding; while the percentages for leaders from middle and lower levels were only 13 and 8 percent respectively.
- Leaders from the upper levels of management accounted for 81 per cent of all outstanding leaders (72 out of 89 leaders). This compares with 17 percent for "Middle" (15 out of 89) levels and only 2 percent for "Lower" levels (2 out of 89).
- The average age of the outstanding leaders was 46 years, compared with 38 and 34 years for the excellent and successful leaders respectively. We used age (rather than years of experience) because we feel that upper-level leaders have occupied several positions on their way up the ladder. Years of experience, on the other hand, could be a poor indicator especially for some people who have occupied fewer positions, doing the same tasks, but for longer periods.

Table 4.2 Accomplishments by level in the organization

Level	Average age	Successful	Excellent	Outstanding	Total (%)
Upper	46	33 (20%)	60 (36%)	72 (44%)	165 (100%)
Middle	38	56 (47%)	48 (40%)	15 (13%)	119 (100%)
Lower	34	15 (58%)	9 (34%)	2 (8%)	26 (100%)
Total	42	104 (33%)	117 (38%)	89 (29%)	310 (100%)

Note: Chi-square = 47.9, df = 4, p = < .01

- Finally, it is noteworthy that 165 out of the total 310 (53 percent) leaders we interviewed occupied senior-level positions in their organizations.

The outstanding leaders we interviewed were exposed to different cultures—and perhaps became more multicultural in their outlook. Our analyses, both quantitative and qualitative (content analysis of interviews), showed that outstanding leaders were positively influenced by a *combination* of one or more of the following events in their lives:

- Working for, or being seconded to, multinational companies
- Working closely with global companies (as partners, customers, suppliers, subcontractors, or through joint ventures)
- Studying overseas
- Extensive travel in the West or Asia
- Working for or with foreign expatriates (as bosses, subordinates, or colleagues; and learning from both benevolent and tough ones).

We simply could not measure the influence that each of these multicultural events had on our leaders; but from content analysis of the answers to our open-ended questions it is reasonable to state that exposure to other cultures (together with other equally important factors) seems to have had a positive impact on leadership success.

All the leaders we interviewed for this study were asked to identify the competencies (talents, skills, and abilities) that were helpful or useful in their careers. They were then asked to tell us in detail about the people and events that have had a lasting impact on them or have shaped their experience of becoming leaders. As we shall see shortly, the outstanding leaders, compared to the others, have attributed their success more to learning from life experiences, commented more frequently about having a strong belief in self-development, and mentioned more people who had an influence on their careers and their success.

In the remainder of this section, we will present some typical examples of the accomplishments by the outstanding leaders, and then present examples of the skills and competencies used by them. The next section will discuss the early years of all the leaders we interviewed, giving examples of the people, events, and other factors that influenced their careers.

Examples of accomplishments by outstanding leaders

Here are some typical examples (actual words with slight editing) that were selected from the accomplishments cited by the outstanding leaders:

"I convinced our European HQ to build a manufacturing plant in Saudi Arabia; it took a few years for the idea to become a reality. Now we a have a successful factory that produces new products."

"I established an architectural model-making division for our company, and I also created a slip-forms construction division (instead of buying one). These two successful entities are my babies: I did them from A to Z."

"Developing nationals: we have exceeded our nationalization target of 50%, and we are now at 53% nationals; this is up from 30% since I became CEO 12 years ago."

"We started holding annual Town Hall meetings for all employees. These meetings (we had to hold several of them because of the large turnout) provide employees with an open forum to discuss the challenges facing them at work and home."

"Our bank's strategy has been very successful; we changed from a traditional local bank to a leading regional bank. Over the years, I recruited around 300 MBAs—now 70% of our recruits are university graduates."

"Implemented a career development program and introduced several tools and methods such as a career assessment center; profiling tests; 360 degrees feedback; and committees to screen potential employees for development purposes."

"Initiated new enhancements in several areas, among them:

- Introduced home ownership allowance for women employees
- Introduced retirement benefits and pensions for widows of deceased retirees
- Established a new performance management program, replacing the old one
- Pushed for hiring more women; we now have 160 Saudi women sponsored by us for higher education."

"I was able to move Human Resources from an administrative support group to a role that adds value to corporate goals and strategy. Now, our recruitment and training strategies are directly linked to corporate short and long-term goals."

"For many years, our Head Office insisted that we invoice our distributors in Swiss Francs; it took some effort to persuade them to invoice in US Dollars, which was linked to local currencies. We saved millions because of this change."

"A short while after joining this company (a food service management company), I introduced a quality department which went on to win the HACCP System certification as a recognition for our dedication to safety and food hygiene."

"Personally established a talent management system (without the help of consultants) whereby we installed the ABC criteria to develop talented people in both leadership positions and experts in technical jobs."

"I changed the mentality for UAE women to be allowed to visit offshore oil fields. I broke the mental barrier by making several one-day visits to meet with employees and observe offshore operations."

"In the last three to four years I am proud of two main initiatives: First, during a major reorganization of the company, I established a Project Management department and a Contract Department.

Secondly, I initiated the start-up of a sister company to support new activities of the holding company."

"After a thorough sales analysis, I initiated a policy to change sales from credit to cash. I convinced top management about changing the old practice, then implemented an action plan, and followed up with it. We saved a lot of money with this change, without any adverse effect on sales."

"Improved safety: My team and I are proud to have set a new safety record of 9 million man hours of work without any lost time injury."

Examples of skills and competencies used by outstanding leaders

When the outstanding leaders were asked: "what talents, skills and abilities helped you in achieving your accomplishments?" they gave a wide range of answers. However, the following were the most helpful and the most frequently mentioned (shown in order of frequency):

- "Recruiting and building an effective team."
- "Working hard and smart."
- "Determination," "tenacity," "dedication," and "persistence."
- "Love and passion for what I do."
- "Always striving to be better than competition through quality and service."
- "Technical knowledge."
- "Wide range of exposure and experiences."
- "Being surrounded by talented people."
- "Ability to deal with people from different cultures or backgrounds."
- "Communication, listening, and convincing skills."
- "Hug and kick!" and "tough love."
- "Honesty and integrity."
- "Balance between long-term and short-term thinking."
- "Taking bold, but calculated, risks."
- "Ability to see the big picture."
- "Being a role model to employees."
- "Flexibility."

- "Delegation skills while holding employees accountable for their decisions."
- "Empowering and delegating."
- "Analytical thinking skills."

We can immediately see that many of the above are simply good managerial skills which can be learned through on-the-job experience or through training and coaching. Others are seemingly learned much earlier in life through good childhood upbringing and education (for example, honesty, passion, and work ethics). It is worth noting that these skills and competencies cited by the outstanding leaders were mentioned less often by excellent and successful leaders.

The early years

People, events, and other factors that influenced careers

We then asked all the leaders whom we interviewed: "How did you develop these talents, skills and abilities?" "Were you born with them? When, how and where did you develop these talents and skills?" As expected, very few respondents said that they were born with the above talents. But even those who said that they were born with such talents quickly added that they had to "polish" and "develop" these inborn talents. Nearly everyone else cited early life experiences, education, work experiences, and other events and people that influenced them. Life is a business school, a few people said. So true!

Table 4.3 shows the most frequently mentioned factors that contributed to success; and the acquisition of their skills and competencies was attributed to these factors by our leaders. Content analysis of the 310 interviews revealed that *people* were the most prominent and most frequently mentioned factors by our leaders. Here are some quotations (exact words, slightly edited or translated) on the three areas that were mentioned most often:

People

"My former manager had a great influence; he allowed me to make mistakes and learn from them."

"My role model is one of my former bosses; he helped push my horizon by giving me extremely challenging responsibilities requiring a lot of leadership skills and personal determination."

Table 4.3   **Factors influencing careers and success**

Influencing factor	Frequency of mention	% of total responses
People:		
Current/previous managers or mentors	174	56
Father	128	41
Mother	65	21
Teacher/professor	22	7
Spouse	19	6
Sibling/relative/friend	16	5
Grandparent	13	4
Events:		
Education (especially extracurricular activities)	118	38
Studying and working overseas (exposure)	89	29
Attending training courses and conferences	87	28
Crises (wars, occupation, personal crisis)	25	8
Early responsibility	24	8
Life experience (learning from mistakes and from success)	15	5
Other factors:		
Working hard	116	37
Gaining experience and knowledge (on the job)	95	30
Reading and self-development	76	24
Luck and opportunities (economic boom, etc.)	26	8
Inborn (personality)	15	5
Religion	7	2
N = 310		

Note: Clearly, many respondents mentioned more than one factor; for example, many of them mentioned both manager and father.

"My former boss, and now a close friend, had tremendous influence on me. He taught me that results are what really count; he 'threw' books at me to read; and he taught me how to be transparent and how to walk the talk."

"My father is my role model; he is a self-made man who taught me honesty, hard work, and self confidence."

"I learned leadership from my father; I saw him leading the family, I watched his behavior during open *majlis* (assembly or visiting room at home); and I worked for him in his factory—I started with cleaning the floors in the factory: started from the bottom."

"My father always put me in leadership positions in situations that even frightened me at the beginning. He also taught me to appreciate people at all levels, from different nationalities and backgrounds."

"Father was a great influence: taught us principles, fairness, and listening to people. He always wanted us to shine."

"My mother instilled in me the love of learning and reading; she gave me lots of books when I was young. She also taught me Math and English."

"The number one influence on my career is my wife. She encouraged me to continue my higher education in the USA years after I started my career. She is always supportive, and she is a big believer in continuous self-development."

"My uncle was my role model—he inspired me to go into engineering and construction. He is a very old man now—I must write and thank him for all he did for me."

"My teacher at the Training Center had a very positive influence on me. He taught me to be patient, to see the big picture, and to think long-term."

It is interesting to note that "Current or previous managers and mentors" had the greatest impact on the leaders we interviewed; this group was mentioned by 56 percent of our respondents (Table 4.3). "Father" and "Mother" were next with 41 percent and 21 percent respectively. However, if we combine "father" and "mother" under the category of "parents," then this group was mentioned by a remarkable 62 percent of respondents, which reconfirms the importance of the early years in the life of potential leaders.

Events

"Being the president of the Arab Students Organization while studying in the USA taught me a lot about leadership—mainly dealing with people, decision making, and politics."

"It was the multicultural environment in the USA, and the responsibility at an early age as a student there."

"The invasion of my country, Kuwait (by Iraq's Saddam Hussein), gave me a reality check; makes you not take things for granted."

"Our family went to France on a vacation, but we were never able to return home to Iraq. My father struggled—seeing him go through being a political refugee was tough, something I'll never forget."

"At the age of 17, I was sentenced to 10 years in prison. Stayed in jail for 5 years, then they deported me (from Palestine) to England. Five years in jail gave me the chance to read and study. I also learned how to deal with tough people, and how to adapt to difficult situations."

"Exposure to life and working in Nigeria, Malaysia, UAE, UK and now Oman; I worked in multi-national workplaces and with different cultures, and this is how I developed my skills."

"I was fortunate to have started my career with a Western bank—I worked for 8 years there during the glorious days of this bank".

"I learned a lot while working for a multinational company overseas; we had to do a lot of presentations to senior management on key issues and decisions."

"Because of the many overseas work assignments in various countries, I became a global 'Bedouin'!"

Outstanding leaders, it seems, were able to learn from adverse events (war, for instance) as well as favorable ones (working for a multinational company or studying abroad). Again and again the ability to learn from life experiences was a key factor that was mentioned often by the outstanding leaders we interviewed.

Other factors

"Reading or being an avid reader": When one of us asked an executive about the one thing that influenced him most, he replied: "Read the framed quote hanging on my office wall". The quote was from Yakub Ibn Ishaq Al-Kindi (ninth-century philosopher):

> We should not be ashamed to acknowledge truth and assimilate it from whatever source it comes to us, even if it is brought to us by former generations and foreign peoples. For him who seeks the truth,

there is nothing of higher value than truth itself; it never cheapens or abases him who searches for it, but ennobles and honors him.

He then asked his secretary to make a photocopy of the quote for us to share with the readers of this book.

"Working hard, but smart; and be passionate about what you do."

"I believe a strong supportive family is a major ingredient of success (especially for entrepreneurs) in this region. This applies to Arabs, Iranians and Asians. The family safety net—both financial and emotional—was a powerful incentive for me to strike out on my own and not fear failure, knowing full well I would never starve!"

"Luck is available for everyone; but you need to put in the effort and jump high to get the fruits of luck."

"Being in the Gulf area during the economic boom, and taking advantage of it. In other words; we were in the right place at the right time."

Box 4.1 Factors that influenced some Western leaders

Great leaders are often interviewed in academic journals and business magazines and are asked to name the events or people in their lives who had an impact on their leadership philosophy or style. The most memorable for us was the coverage in a special issue of *Harvard Business Review*, where 17 leaders in business, academia, and the arts were asked about the experiences in their lives that taught them the most about leadership. Their answers were fascinating, but not surprising. Compare their words with the responses we received from the leaders we interviewed. Here are some brief excerpts from what six of them said:

Percy Barnevik, former chairman and CEO of ABB, Switzerland

(His mentor): "He was extremely determined and forceful, and he drove his people hard to accomplish what he wanted to get done. But they were very loyal to him because he somehow was able to combine an iron-fist style with a positive and enjoyable atmosphere."

Chris Argyris, Professor Emeritus of Education and Organizational Behavior at Harvard Business School

(Infantry lieutenant): "I suppose his kind of uncompromising commitment would be called tough love today. To me it's a powerful reminder that leadership is about maximizing your follower's well-being, not their comfort."

Jack Welch, Former chairman and CEO of General Electric

(His mother): "My mother taught me about unconditional love, at the same time, set very tough standards for achievement. That combination of 'hugs and kicks' brought out the best in me, and I used it myself to bring out the best in others."

Anne Mulcahy, President and CEO of Xerox

(Her father): "I learned some of my most valuable lessons in leadership at the family dinner table, where my father presided over nightly debates with me, my mother, and four brothers. ... [He] knew exactly how to extract independent thinking and creative ideas from all of us. ... And we didn't just debate; my father encouraged us to turn our words into action."

James Conlon, Conductor of the Paris Opera and the general music director of the city of Cologne, Germany

(Dr. Martin Luther King, Jr.): "When I was 12 years old, my father took me to hear Dr. King speak at a luncheon. ... His dedication, bravery, and altruism were a tremendous inspiration, but it was his death that had the most profound effect on me. ... King's inspiration and clear moral vision have helped me throughout my entire life to differentiate between depth and superficiality, between the important and the trivial."

Dick Brown, Chairman and CEO of EDS, US

(His parents): "I trace my leadership philosophy to my mother and father. My father was the decision maker and disciplinarian in the family. My mother was gregarious and affable, and she was always able to find the best in people. She was a terrific motivator and energy supplier. I try to blend the best of both of them by having a disposition that's rooted in realism while keeping my compass pointed on the positive side of human nature."

Source: Harvard Business Review (2001), pp. 27–38.

The early ingredients for success

After asking probing questions to find what factors, people, events or experiences contributed to their success, we then asked each of the 310 managers to rank in order of importance the same ten ingredients of success that were discovered in the Meirc study (1989) and later confirmed by Muna (2003). The ranking process reconfirmed and lent more credibility to the open-ended questions that we probed at the beginning of the interviews. Table 4.4 shows the results for 2010, and compares them to rankings of 1989 and 2003. Using Friedman's test

Table 4.4 **Ten ingredients for success; For 12 countries (6 GCC countries and 6 Northern Arab countries); 2010 ranking compared with the 2003 and 1989 studies**

Ranking	Mean rank	Ingredient for success		
2010 Ranking (N = 310)			2003 Ranking (N = 181)	1989 Ranking (N = 140)
1	3.5	Self-development	2	5
2	4.4	Ethics and values	3	4
3	4.5	The knowledge base (job experience)	5	8
4	4.9	Quality of education	1	1
5	5.1	Early responsibility	4	3
6	5.2	Exposure and role models	6	2
7	6.0	Standards and feedback (by manager)	10	7
8	6.4	Training opportunities	7	6
9	6.9	A problem-solving culture	8	10
10	8.2	Formal career development	9	9

Analyses of 2010 rankings:

1. Mean rank (out of 10): total ranking score divided by total number of respondents.
2. Friedman and Kendall's W tests show significant agreement among the respondents on the ranking of the ten ingredients:

   Kendall's W = .208, chi-square = 581.5, df = 9, p. = 0.000

3. Factor analysis of the ten ingredients showed that there were no specific groups of variables that can explain the variation in the data. There were some large and significant correlations among the ten variables or ingredients; see Table A.9b: Correlation Matrix, which shows the correlations and the 1-tailed significance levels for the top six ingredients.

For the statistical analyses of the above data, we are grateful to Dr. Harold E. Dyck, Professor of Information and Decision Sciences at California State University, San Bernardino.

and Kendall's W test, we found that there was significant agreement among the leaders on the ranking of the ten ingredients (Kendall's W = .208, chi-square = 581.5, df = 9, p. = 0.000). For a more detailed statistical analysis, see Appendix A.

Again, the results are fascinating and enlightening. Their implications for recruitment and selection are even more enormous: we found that for many of the respondents, their talents, skills, and abilities were developed early in life, well before they started their work careers; they were developed during their childhood and during the years they spent in school and university, see Table 4.4. For a large number of our respondents, development was further enhanced early on in their careers by either gaining practical expertise through work (ranked 3) or having great bosses (ranked 7). In short, the factors that lead to success are developed early in life, modified and fortified through life experience, and lived out in work and personal experiences.

We discovered, like others before us, that the early paths to success begin in childhood and continue to the time most potential leaders start their organizational careers in their early twenties. The exception was knowledge base (job experience and technical knowledge), which was ranked third in terms of importance and was the one that is partly acquired through education and partly through job experience after one starts a career. An early word of caution: it is very unlikely (but not necessary) that potential leaders will have been greatly influenced by every one of those ingredients.

The top five ingredients (out of the top six) that shaped potential leaders early on during childhood and up to the time they started a career were:

1. *Self-development*: Self-development is manifested by an insatiable thirst for learning and by a passion for continuous development—throughout life. A large number of our respondents described themselves as avid readers. They also described themselves as good listeners. Curiosity is one of the basic ingredients of leadership, according to Warren Bennis.
2. *Ethics and values*: This highly ranked ingredient refers to the inculcation of work ethics and values by parents, relatives, peers, or teachers. Leadership, we are told by many writers, requires integrity, passion, determination and persistence, commitment to quality work, and respect for others. These attributes of leadership cannot possibly be

taught when people are in their mid-twenties or thirties. It might be, we believe, too late then; hence, the more vital that child upbringing becomes as an ingredient to the making of potential leaders.

3. *Early responsibility*: Early responsibility, whether at home or work, inculcates work ethics and values as well as responsibility and accountability. Again, several of the interviewees mentioned that early responsibility was imposed upon them due to personal or family traumas and crises. The luckier ones were deliberately given early responsibility by their parents at a young age, increasing the responsibilities as the children grew.

4. *Quality of education*: The quality of education refers not so much to the grades obtained in high school or university, but mainly to the extracurricular activities that a person engages in during his or her educational period (sports, student associations and clubs, charitable or environmental activities, theater and music, and so on). Many of the leadership competencies such as teamwork, social and emotional skills, and followership are learned at school or university. Quality of education also refers to the acquisition of analytical and creative thinking, the stretching of the mind, communication skills, and the social interactions with high caliber students and teachers.

5. *Exposure and role models*: This ingredient refers to the process of learning from others through exposure and role models. Learning by exposure to different people and cultures widens the horizon of the young. Many of the respondents who studied or worked abroad mentioned the favorable impact of being exposed to a different culture. Learning from persons you respect and admire (role models) encourages people to excel long after such role models are gone. Many leaders we spoke with were, and still are, inspired by their role models.

After analyzing the responses of the 310 leaders in more detail, a few observations are in order:

1. Self-development was ranked the highest in terms of importance by the leaders we interviewed, with an average of 3.5 out of 10, as shown in Table 4.4. One out of four leaders ranked self-development as the most important ingredient for their success.

2. All three categories of leaders ranked self-development as the most important to their careers: successful leaders (3.3 out of ten), excellent leaders (3.8 out of ten), and outstanding leaders (3.4 out of ten).

3. The knowledge base climbed to third place from fifth place in 2003 and from eighth place in the 1989 study. Thus, technical job knowledge and job experience have become more crucial to success than was observed 21 years ago. This is partly explained by the larger number of women leaders who participated in the 2010 study, who gave significantly more weight to this ingredient than men leaders.

4. Quality of education dropped from first place to fourth. A remarkable 95 percent of the leaders interviewed held university degrees; as compared to 87 percent 21 years ago. Could this drop from first to fourth be partly explained by the interesting fact that 44 percent of our respondents held a Masters or higher degrees, as compared to 28 percent in 1989? Interestingly, the older the leader, the less weight they give to this ingredient. Equally interesting, 53 percent of all leaders studied abroad and obtained their first or second degrees from Western universities, mostly from the US and UK. This is a significant decrease from the 66 percent who studied abroad among those who participated in our 1989 study.

5. There were no statistically significant differences in the overall rankings of the ten ingredients by leaders from GCC countries and leaders from Northern Arab countries; or by other variables such as nationality, educational background, size of organization, or type of business.

Because self-development was the most highly ranked ingredient in the making of leaders, and because it is a lifelong endeavor, we considered it as one of the five paths to outstanding leadership. These five paths are available for potential leaders to choose from on their journey to become outstanding managers once they start their careers. Some outstanding leaders used one or two paths, while some used all five paths. Four of these paths are discussed in the next chapter; the fifth path, cultivating emotional intelligence competencies, is covered in Chapter 6.

5
Paths to Outstanding Leadership

Being busy does not always mean work. The object of all work is production or accomplishments, and to either of these ends there must be forethought, system, planning, intelligence, and honest purpose, as well as perspiration.

—*Thomas Edison*

Hard work beats talent when talent doesn't work hard.
—*Tim Notke*

There are truths on this side of the Pyrenees that are falsehoods on the other.
—*Blaise Pascal*

Potential leaders who are fortunate enough to acquire the basic ingredients of leadership during their early years (ingredients such as good education and early experiences; upbringing; work ethics and values—see Figure 3.1) will still have a few more paths to follow on their journey toward becoming outstanding leaders. We will examine a number of specific actions that potential leaders and their organizations must undertake to enhance the likelihood of future success when we discuss these four paths:

Path 1: Working hard and smart
Path 2: Training and career development

Path 3: Personal development
Path 4: Cultural sensitivity

The subject of cultural sensitivity (Path 4) will be discussed at greater length because we strongly believe that it is a critical competency for leaders who are doing business at the global level, or who are working overseas, or with employees (or followers), customers, suppliers and other people who come from different cultures and countries.

Paths 1, 2, 3 have been covered in depth in the academic and popular literature; therefore, we will present in this chapter only the salient points on these paths while weaving in some of our research findings, including quotations from the outstanding leaders we interviewed.

Chapter 6, "Learning to Lead," examines Path 5: cultivating the emotional intelligence competencies required for leadership success.

Path 1: Working hard and smart

We took notice when 37 percent of interviewees (Table 4.3) attributed leadership success to "working hard." This is what many of them said when they were asked to elaborate:

–Working hard, but smart
–Having a deep passion for the idea or mission
–Determination
–Perseverance and patience
–Persistence
–Being results-oriented, or being obsessed with getting results
–Working hard on getting my people to share my dreams or objectives.

Very few, if any, said that working hard means working long hours or more days. Working hard, it seems, is a combination of determination, endurance, perseverance, resilience, and working smarter. The words "passion" and "passionate" were frequently mentioned by many of the leaders we talked with.

We think that Thomas Edison got it right in the above quote when he said the purpose of work is accomplishments, and it requires forethought, planning, intelligence, purpose, and perspiration. Yet we came across a very small number of managers who said that working hard was a critical factor in their success, but they had very few outstanding accomplishments to show for it. Working hard with purpose and with result-orientation is apparently what really counts. One CEO told us, "I am results-oriented, but one must deliver the results through his people."

We are told that successful leaders are those who "do the right things," while managers "do things right" (Bennis, 1989). But perhaps as important is that successful leaders are results-oriented: they are determined to do the right things in order to achieve the desired results. They do smart things that make "the right" things happen. Determination, persistence and perseverance are great attributes *only if* we are fairly clear about the desired results. One of Stephen Covey's seven habits is "Begin with the end in mind" (Covey, 1989), regardless of whether the desired result is achieving a personal mission or organizational strategy, medium-term objective, or short-term goal. Jim Collins (2001) wrote that great leadership (Level 5 leadership) "is not just about humility and modesty. It is equally about ferocious resolve, an almost stoic determination to do whatever needs to be done to make the organization great."

We also like the definition of determination that was provided by Edward de Bono who wrote that determination is indicated by single-mindedness, persistence and a strong sense of direction. He calls this type of determination "a little madness." We like it because so many of the outstanding leaders we spoke with used similar words when describing "working hard."

The founder of Nuqul Group, a successful Jordanian conglomerate, feels it is often sheer will and determination that induce and drive success. He describes his own experience with these words:

> While good organizational skills, discipline, and sustainability of energy levels are central to the ability to work on multiple projects, it is the urge to create something that enables you to do it. It may be hard to believe this, but what helped me on the road to success was this urge, which is omnipresent, deep inside me, in my brain, in my body, and has accompanied me throughout my career."
>
> (Wheatcroft and Hawatmeh, 2008)

Finally, working hard and smart is particularly effective when a person has the ability to continuously "put things in perspective";

to see the forest for the trees; or what a major oil company called the "Helicopter View"—the ability to see the "Big Picture." This is one of the leadership skills that can be learned at any age, and one that was mentioned often in the interviews.

"You need to be passionate about what you believe in and what you do."

"You need to keep in mind the big picture while you focus on the details."

"My success was due to working hard on getting my people to share my dreams, my vision."

"Think long-term, but always achieve results while on the way to your ultimate objectives."

Path 2: Training and career development

When we asked, in an open-ended question, how they developed their skills and abilities 30 per cent of the respondents said that gaining job experience and knowledge was one of the keys to their success (Table 4.3). They also ranked it third among the ten ingredients that were presented to them (Table 4.4). Such valuable experience and knowledge is slowly acquired in several ways: on-the-job learning, off-the-job training, attending meetings and conferences, coaching, carrying out special projects, rotational assignments, to name just a few. These planned events, we believe, represent developmental paths that potential leaders have to take from time to time on their journey to success.

Gaining the right skills and knowledge requires challenging developmental assignments and the opportunity to learn new skills as a person progresses through various levels in the organization. Again and again the respondents in this research study attributed their accomplishments and success to skills accumulated over relatively long periods of time, spent in different and challenging areas of responsibilities and environments; and they learned from their successes as well as their failures. Having a coach or a wise mentor, many respondents said, was extremely helpful—especially if he or she gave stretching assignments and provided constructive feedback. Having a supportive boss was a key to success for 56 percent of our respondents (see Table 4.3). Interestingly, a few mentioned that they were influenced by having "terrible" or "weak" bosses, and that they leaned from the mistakes of such bosses!

In the US, Ulrich and his co-authors (2008) discuss a 2006 study conducted by the Learning and Development Roundtable titled "Leaders Who Develop Leaders: Establishing the Foundations of Effective Leader-Led Development." The study found that senior Human Resource (HR) executives rated these three developmental activities as the most effective:

1. Coaching provided by the leader's direct manager;
2. Job rotations and assignments; and
3. Action learning.

It appears that coaching or mentoring provided by the direct manager has been extremely beneficial to a large number of the leaders we interviewed for this book. However, this coaching was informal, ad hoc, and sometimes unintended. HR professionals, it seems, need to be more proactive in designing and implementing coaching and/or mentoring programs. We know of several oil and gas companies in the Gulf that successfully run such programs for their national employees.

HR professionals, supported by top management, can play an important role in another important area. They are expected to design and implement performance management systems that serve three purposes: performance evaluation and appraisal; identification of training needs; and systematic identification of employees with high potential. Of course, HR professionals facilitate these three separate processes in close partnership with top and line managers. Performance appraisal is a vast subject, which is best left for other books to cover. Training needs are fairly easy to identify and there are several tools that are available to both HR professionals and line managers to correctly identify the necessary training to fill gaps in skills and knowledge. Identification of high potential employees, however, is a more complicated and controversial matter. It impacts the long-term development of careers and must be linked to the long-term strategy of the organization.

A common error sometimes made by both HR professionals and line managers is their failure to differentiate between high performance and high potential. A hard-working employee whose work performance is excellent is often quickly and mistakenly recommended for promotion and added responsibilities. However, promoting hard-working employees just because of their high performance and without adequate training and career development may result in fulfilling Peter's Principle: in a hierarchy every employee tends to rise to his or her level of incompetence. Promotions, when vacancies are available, should go to those employees who have demonstrated both high performance and high potential for at least two or three years in a row. In short, "high flyers," "stars," or "employees on a fast track" are talented, competent, hard-working people who should have specially designed career development programs to get them ready for higher positions.

Successful and large multinational companies ensure continuity of available leaders (their bench strength) by carefully selecting potential leaders from their pools of talent, and provide the talented leaders with management and career development plans, which are linked to their succession planning. Witness, for example, the practices of GE with their famous 20-70-10 differentiation of their employees (20 percent are A's); or, Unilever's "high potential" pool of around 20 percent; or Procter and Gamble's "Talent Portfolio" where replacements for key leadership positions are the concern of not only the CEO and HR, but involves active input from the board of directors. More will be said about this critical subject in Chapter 9.

The questions that face the potential leader are these: "What if my organization does not have career development systems?" "What can I do?" Here are some more rugged paths that may be followed:

- Design your own career development plan—even if you have to enlist help from an outside HR expert on career development. Once your plan is designed, work hard and lobby for its implementation. There are no easy answers to the question of which developmental activities are best; each person's plan will be tailored to fit that person and his or her specific or unique work environment. We shall suggest some developmental activities in the next section, when we discuss the closely interrelated topic of Personal Development.

- Get on the radar screen, as Jack Welch (2005) advised in his book *Winning*. "Do deliver sensational performance, far beyond expectations, and at every opportunity expand your job beyond its official boundaries." Welch elaborated:

> But an even more effective way to get promoted is to expand your job's horizons to include bold and unexpected activities. Come up with a new concept or process that doesn't improve just your results, but your unit's results and the company's overall performance. Change your job in a way that makes the people around you work better and your boss look smarter. Don't just do the predictable.

Getting on the radar screen also means being an early champion of major projects or initiatives. Welch writes: "The best proof of the radar screen dynamic is in the numbers. Today, more than half of the senior vice presidents reporting to Jeff Immelt have worked in global assignments, and one-third of the company's approximately 180 officers have significant Six Sigma experience."

Welch's advice brought back to memory the findings of the earlier Meirc (1989) study, when a number of outstanding Gulf managers told us: "Responsibility (or authority) is grabbed rather than given." Being proactive, it seems, works well for many people. The following words from some of the leaders who participated in this current study demonstrate this proactive attitude:

"The harder you work, the more opportunities you create, the luckier you become."

"Seek challenges: don't go for the easy work; aim high."

"I've always been willing to walk the extra mile ... recognition follows."

Path 3: Personal development

The third path, which is closely related to the previous one, comes into play when an organization is not particularly good at providing its employees with sufficient training or career development. The individual has to take charge of his or her own development. The late Peter Drucker believed that "development is always self-development."

He also believed that responsibility for development has shifted from the company to the individual. In a 1999 article, he wisely wrote:

> We live in an age of unprecedented opportunity: if you've got ambition and smarts, you can rise to the top of your chosen profession, regardless of where you started out.
>
> But with opportunity comes responsibility. Companies today aren't managing their employees' careers; knowledge workers must, effectively, be their own chief executive officers. It's up to you to carve out your place, to know when to change course, and to keep yourself engaged and productive during a work life that may span some 50 years. To do those things well, you'll need to cultivate a deep understanding of yourself—not only what your strengths and weaknesses are but also how you learn, how you work with others, what your values are, and where you can make the greatest contribution. Because only when you operate from strengths can you achieve true excellence.
>
> (Drucker, 1999)

Managing oneself, according to Drucker, revolves around some basic principles. It is up to the person to ask questions about how he or she thinks and works and then seek answers. One must then act on these answers; Drucker has found people rarely do. He urged leaders to identify their strengths and to identify areas where they can improve, and to make new contributions to their organization. Drucker believed that the failure to do these things leads to ineffectiveness.

Our research findings suggested that self-development was a key to leadership success. Self-development ranked the highest of the ten ingredients to success among the 310 people we interviewed. But more significantly, the content analysis of the answers to open-ended questions showed that continuous learning was a significant contributing factor for 24 percent of the leaders we interviewed. Not only did they cite self-development as an important ingredient to their own success, but they also mentioned it as frequently when asked to give advice to younger, future leaders. Here are some examples of the advice they gave to the young future leaders:

"Never stop self development: listen and learn, read and learn, do and learn."

"Continue to stay strong through continuous learning. Have an active inquiring mind."

"Learn from your mistakes."

"Always learn ... never stop learning... especially from your juniors."

"I read a lot even from the days I was young, and I always strive for learning. That's my advice to younger people."

When one hears the term self-development, two things come to mind. First, it is a process to enhance one's skills, knowledge, and competencies in order to improve work performance, or to achieve future career aspirations. Second, the initiative comes from the person himself. In other words, one must take personal responsibility for planning and implementing a strategy to develop oneself throughout life.

For any self-development to take place a person must first and foremost be highly motivated to bring about the desired change; additionally, a person must know himself well. During the interviews, we were reminded that the Holy Quran exhorts people to seek change: "Verily never will God change the condition of a people until they change it themselves" (13:11). The other prerequisite for self-development comes from Greek philosophy: "Know Thyself." Knowing oneself means to truthfully analyze one's own strengths, and to acknowledge areas for improvements taking into account career aspiration, including personal values and objectives.

A potential leader may have to seek help from HR professionals (insiders or outsiders) who specialize in career development and who are experienced in designing learning plans. A learning plan may include any or most of the following developmental activities:

- seek and solicit advice from a mentor (from within or outside the organization),
- ask for rotational assignments,
- take advantage of on-the-job training opportunities,
- volunteer for special projects, task forces or teams,
- attend meaningful training programs, conferences, workshops, and talks by visiting speakers,
- read widely, including relevant literature and journals (use the Internet),
- attend meetings with the intention of asking questions and learning from others,

- grab uncontested tasks or responsibilities,
- visit similar organizations or industries with the aim of learning best practices,
- join professional associations or clubs,
- enroll in higher education programs (even if part-time or distant learning),
- take advantage of e-learning (if available in your organization).

Of course, a learning plan has to be scheduled over time; some of the developmental activities will be ongoing, others will have to be planned for certain times or specific periods over the coming years. Finally, periodic reviews of the learning plan are necessary to evaluate whether learning has indeed taken place; it is similar to measuring progress and success from time to time. Once again, there must be an insatiable thirst, a burning desire, for more knowledge and continuous learning throughout life. If you are truly self-motivated, learning can take place from the cradle to the grave.

Once more, if a leader is determined, persistent, and lucky, he or she can benefit greatly from finding a wise mentor or a coach. Warren Bennis suggested that young leaders should "recruit" their mentors. He writes, "While the popular view of mentors is that they seek out younger people to encourage and champion, in fact the reverse is more often true. The best mentors are usually recruited, and one mark of a future leader is the ability to identify, woo, and win the mentors who will change his or her life" (Bennis, 2004).

Lastly, it is only appropriate at this point to quote Charles Handy from a commentary he made in *The Making of Gulf Managers* (Meirc, 1989). He wrote, "The path to success is built on learning. It starts with a good education and continues if, and perhaps only if, it leads into an organization which has a culture of learning and if the individual who treads the path is consumed with a passion to learn." Fortunately, we did interview a number of leaders who were lucky to have both ingredients: a passion to learn and an organization with a culture of learning.

Path 4: Cultural sensitivity

Over the past 20 years, we have tracked how expatriates working in the six GCC countries are perceived by their hosts (Meirc, 1989; Muna, 2003). More specifically, we asked respondents to tell us what characteristics they admired most, and what characteristics they disliked most about Western expatriates, Arab expatriates, and Asian expatriates. That is precisely what we did again in this current field research. Additionally, we asked: "What are the most challenging aspects of working with multinational organizations?" In brief, we discovered that cultural differences require leaders who work in multicultural settings to have one additional, often over-looked, competency: a high level of cultural sensitivity that allows leaders to bridge cultures and achieve mutually beneficial long-term results.

In this section we shall first present the research findings on per-ception of expatriates, and later attempt to answer two important questions: Does national culture matter when organizations employ many different nationalities, as a large number of them do in the GCC countries (Saudi Aramco has employees from around 60 differ-ent countries)? Does national culture matter when organizations are doing business across the globe?

The research findings on perception of expatriates

How are expatriates perceived by their hosts? For the purpose of our research, we classified expatriates in three categories: *Western* expatriates, mostly from Europe; *Arab* expatriates; and *Asian* expa-triates, mostly from the Indian subcontinent and Philippines. It is important to note at the outset that many respondents felt their answers did not necessarily apply to all Western, or all Arab, or all Asian expatriates. Many qualified their statements by saying: "If I were to generalize, these are the characteristics which I admire most." Examples of the characteristics, which they disliked, were similarly qualified.

The most striking observation about the recent findings is that they have not changed much over the past 20 years. Most of the characteristics shown below were mentioned in the earlier studies. Tables 5.1 and 5.2 show a summary of the perceptions, listed in the order of frequency of mention. Respondents were asked to men-tion up to three characteristics that they admired and three that they disliked. We tried as much as possible to keep the exact words that were used by the respondents to describe these characteristics. Shown below are the top five characteristics for each expatriate group.

Table 5.1   **Perception of expatriates: Most admired characteristics (as mentioned by % of respondents)**

Western expatriates
1. Professionalism (25%)
2. Organized, systematic, process-oriented, and attention to details (23%)
3. Respect for time and deadlines, and punctuality (19%)
4. Know-how, expertise, and international experience (17%)
5. Straight forward, direct, open and frank (16%)
(All five characteristics appeared in the earlier studies, but in a slightly different order.)

Arab expatriates
1. Same culture, language and habits (37%)
2. Friendly, warm, approachable, sociable, easy-going (27%)
3. Loyalty and trustworthiness (17%)
4. Hard workers/dedicated (15%)
5. Good learners/develop themselves (6%)*
(Did not make the top five this time: Decisiveness.)

Asian expatriates
1. Hard workers/ dedicated soldiers (53%)
2. Disciplined and follow guidelines/instructions (16%)
3. Competent, especially for administrative and technical jobs (10%)
4. Loyalty (8%)*
5. Respectful and friendly (7%)
(Did not make the top five this time: Perseverance).

N = 310

Note: * = New to the list.

These findings, we believe, tell us as much about the host managers we interviewed for this book as they do about the expatriates. Perhaps one can speculate that the most admired characteristics are those that host organizations would like to see more of in their own national employees. This is indeed the explanation given by most participants who have attended our seminars when presented with the findings of the earlier studies.

The most disturbing finding is the negative perception host managers have about Western expatriates: the disliked characteristics are directly linked to cultural differences or lack of understanding of cultures (see Table 5.2), especially the top two interrelated characteristics, which if combined, totaled a remarkable 68 percent of the responses. This does not augur well for mutual trust, teamwork, or

Table 5.2 Perception of expatriates: Most disliked characteristics (as mentioned by % of respondents)

Western expatriates
1. Superiority complex and arrogance (42%)
2. Lack of understanding or respect for local culture or way of life (26%)
3. Not flexible, "trapped in their boxes," and "my way is the best way" (9%)*
4. Cliquish, no desire to mix with other nationalities (at or outside work) (8%)
5. Cold, aloof, and unemotional (8%)*
(Characteristics that did not make the top five this time: materialistic; and opposition to the training and development of national employees.)

Arab expatriates
1. Low value for time, poor punctuality (16%)
2. Too emotional, sensitive to criticism, take things personally (12%)
3. Lack of transparency, deceiving, and hidden agendas (10%)*
4. Weak planning and organizational skills (8%)
5. Mixing business with personal affairs (6%)*
(Did not make the top five this time: cliquish; and hinder development of nationals.)

Asian expatriates
1. Overly obedient, passive, do not stand up for their ideas (17%)
2. Cliquish "mafia" type (14%)
3. Reluctant to take responsibility and to make decisions (13%)*
4. Low on creativity and innovation (especially at lower levels) (10%)
5. Weak on leadership skills, are better as followers (7%)
(Did not make the top five this time: hinder development of nationals, by blocking knowledge and information).

N = 310

Note: * = New to the list.

motivation—given that most Western expatriates hold middle to high positions in these organizations. It seems that both host managers and Western expatriates could benefit from cultural awareness training aimed at improving cross-cultural skills and enhancing cultural empathy. Hence the importance of cultural sensitivity for both parties and the need to build bridges across cultures, a crucial topic that will be discussed at length shortly.

The readers will notice that one common disliked characteristic for all categories of expatriates did not make the top five in this current research, namely, hindering, or opposition to, training and development of national employees. This is a healthy sign that is perhaps explained by the fact that senior management in most GCC organizations are nowadays local nationals, and that training and developing nationals have become a much higher priority in the past decade, at the governmental and organizational levels.

Bridging cultures

Culture, according to most definitions, is the way in which people and societies behave based on their beliefs, values, norms, customs, and attitudes. These components of culture are usually deeply rooted in history, religion, traditions, and philosophy. In a nutshell, culture is a way of life. "Worldly" managers and leaders are those who can manage with relative ease across cultural boundaries, be they departmental, corporate, or national cultures. The term "worldly mindset" is borrowed from Mintzberg (2004); it is rather different from "global mindset" in that it refers to the experiences in life which enable one to understand, respect, and work well with cultural differences. Global mindset, on the other hand, implies convergence over time toward a common, homogeneous, and universal culture—with a hint of superiority for one's own culture or economic beliefs. Although the technological and information revolution has shrunk the globe, cultural differences endure.

A visit to another country (or for that matter a visit within a country) will quickly reveal cultural differences. Such differences must be understood and bridged. Here "cultural differences" refer not to the differences in artifacts or cultural symbols one encounters at first sight, such as houses and monuments, eating habits, dress codes,[1] and outwardly daily behavior. These aspects are easy to understand and can be learned during short country-specific seminars. Such differences are merely the *outer* layers of culture, and are often the ones that are constantly changing and are likely to be exported widely; for instance, people globally can be found wearing jeans, using the Internet and mobile phones, and eating fast food. One needs to peel the outer layers of the onion to better understand cultural differences.

The onion metaphor was used by Hofstede (2001) and by Trompenaars and Hamden-Turner (1997) to depict the various layers of culture. It is the inner layers of the onion that represent values and norms—the core—of the culture (see Figure 5.1). Here one finds

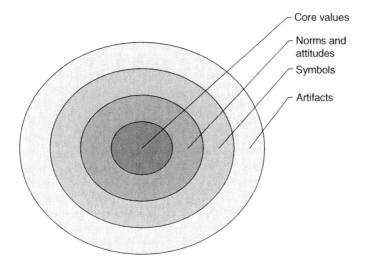

Figure 5.1   **Culture as an onion**

a culture's definition of what is good versus bad, right versus wrong, normal versus abnormal, moral versus immoral, and so forth. These values and norms are deep seated and have their origins in history and traditions, religion, philosophy, legal system, geography, and the economic milieu. Moreover, these core values are relatively stable and enduring; therefore, they are much more difficult to influence— a point worth keeping in mind when interacting and working with people from other cultures.

We like the metaphor "culture as an onion." Onions, like cultures, come in different varieties, shapes, flavors, and colors; interestingly, the color of the core permeates each layer. If one is not skilled at slicing and peeling an onion, it can cause eye irritation and bring tears to the eyes. In the case of a skilled person, irritation and tears may still happen. Similarly, when crossing borders and cultures, an overseas traveler or a business executive must learn the skills of bridging cultures and becoming culturally sensitive.

Cultural differences, however, lead some people to believe that "if it's different from my own culture, it is probably wrong." This ethnocentric view could be damaging to relations whether on the international, regional, or organizational level, and it is certainly counterproductive to doing business globally. This view stems from an unconscious reference to one's own cultural values, experiences, and knowledge as a basis for decisions, also known as Self-Reference Criterion (SRC). SRC is closely connected to ethnocentrism, that is, the notion that one's own culture (and thus one's company) knows best how to do things. Instead, what is required from tomorrow's worldly leaders are the competencies (skills, knowledge, and attitudes) to bridge cultural differences through mutual understanding, respect and tolerance.

Another mistake often made by managers working overseas is to attribute talent and intelligence to national employees based on how well they spoke the language of the expatriate manager. For example, during our experience of designing career development programs for national employees in the GCC countries (Bahrain, Kuwait, Oman, Saudi Arabia, Qatar and UAE), we found that many Western expatriate managers would be heavily influenced by the nationals' ability to speak English or French and would rate them as "high potential" employees because of their social speaking skills! And, in some cases, nationals wearing smart Western dress would get a more favorable estimate of their potential as future managers!

This bias is not restricted to Western expatriates. Some Arab executives and managers looked more favorably toward Western consultants when awarding management consulting contracts in the belief that "Western/foreign" expertise is better than local or Arab. Our own firm, Meirc Training & Consulting, had to work very hard for years to dispel that bias. Our experience, repeated many times over the years, has been to obtain management consulting assignments (at lower fees) in order to rework or fix the work carried out by foreign consulting firms who failed simply because they did not take culture into account when they took on consulting projects.

The same phenomenon often occurred in the area of management training. Some Western training firms unfamiliar with Middle Eastern culture were not very successful because their seminar leaders would focus on, for example, labor unions negotiations, diversity at work, and "participative" managerial styles; issues which are not applicable or not culturally relevant to the region. Our firm was able to succeed in consulting and training assignments mainly because we recruit bicultural and bilingual consultants who have studied and worked in both the West and in the Middle East, and thus are able to bridge cultures and know which Western management styles and techniques work well in the Gulf region, and which do not.

Another critical skill of a culturally sensitive leader is to build mutual trust with foreign counterparts in order to carry out mutually beneficial transactions on a long-term basis. In many cultures, this trust is built slowly over time, somewhat like having an engagement before marriage. What if one does not have time to build trust? The solution, in many cases, is to use personal connections and contacts. Personal connections are very important to doing business all over the world, but in some parts of the world they are essential. In the Middle East the Arabic word for connections is *wastah*. In small, close-knit societies *wastah* still plays a very important role. In Japan it is called *kone*. In China it is known as *guanxi*. For example, Kambil and his colleagues (2006) maintain that a prerequisite to doing business in China is knowledge and appreciation of the importance of *guanxi*—an effective use of social networks to advance business relations. They wrote, "Although its role is often misunderstood in the West, *guanxi* is widely seen as crucial to business relationships in China, where important business transactions are rarely conducted between strangers. *Guanxi* relies on social capital drawn from personal contacts, which bridges critical information gaps, enabling favors based on trust or mutual benefit."

Since communication is so essential to doing business across cultures, it is critical to pay particular attention to the differences in communication between "high-context" and "low-context" cultures, terms popularized long ago by Edward Hall (1971). Western countries tend to be low-context, while Eastern ones are high-context. LeBaron (2003) writing about communication and cultural fluency stated that all of us engage in both high-context and low-context communication. She added that at times we "say what we mean, and mean what we say" leaving little to be "read into" the explicit message. This is low-context communication. At other times, the messages that we want to convey are sent by nonverbal cues, or we may infer and imply these messages without speaking them directly. This is high-context communication. Most of the time, we are somewhere in the middle of the continuum, relying to some extent on context, but also on the literal meaning of words. The following points are taken from LeBaron's book:

Generally, low-context communicators from the West interacting with high-context communicators from the East should be mindful that

- nonverbal messages and gestures may be as important as what is said;
- status and identity may be communicated nonverbally and require appropriate acknowledgement; and
- face-saving and tact may be important, and need to be balanced with the desire to communicate fully and frankly.

High-context communicators from the East interacting with low-context communicators from the West should be mindful that

- things can be taken at face value rather than comprising layers of meaning;
- roles and functions may be decoupled from status and identity;
- direct questions and observations are not necessarily meant to offend, but to clarify and advance shared goals; and
- indirect cues may not be enough to get the other's attention.

Another way to describe those differences in cross-cultural communication is to remember Peter Drucker's statement that "the most important thing in communication is to hear what isn't being said." Western expatriates and business people as well as Middle Eastern managers would do well to become aware of these cultural differences to avoid some of the harmful perceptions that we witnessed earlier (Table 5.2); perceptions such as that of displaying "superiority complex and arrogance," being "cold and aloof," or "overly obedient."

The single most important challenge in building cultural bridges is to become a student of the culture in which one is interested. As an example, let us use the challenge of becoming computer literate. If learning computer skills is essential for success, then one's mindset would be "don't allow computer literacy to stand in your way!" The same, we believe, is true of learning about a new culture: "don't let culture stand in your way!" Acknowledge the new culture by learning about it, by not allowing it to be a barrier, or not allowing it to stand in the way of your success. This mindset is the opposite of ignoring culture or dismissing it as being irrelevant or "wrong."

Becoming culturally sensitive involves immersion in a new culture:

- Reading and learning about the outer as well as the inner layers of the onion (cultural values, norms, and their sources);
- Reaching out to better understand the context and circumstances of other cultures before making judgments about what is right or wrong, and what is good or bad; in short, being open-minded and non-judgmental;
- Interacting empathetically with its people. Remember one of Covey's 7 habits is: "seek first to understand, then to be understood." (Covey, 1989);
- Looking at differences as opportunities to bridge the gulf between cultures (finding common ground in apparent differences);
- Acting toward the mutual benefits of both parties (without "going native"); and
- Finally, and perhaps most important, having the ability and willingness to continuously learn from the enriching experience of working and living in different cultures.

In the final analysis, bridging cultures means the ability to transcend those surmountable differences that will continue to exist between national cultures—just like we are able to transcend differences that exist between individuals, groups, and organizations of the same culture. If one is able to take a global snapshot of the business world at any time during the first part of the twenty-first century, we would venture to say that it will probably look like Figure 5.2, depending on which looking glasses are used.

Here is a hypothetical, but very realistic, example to clarify Figure 5.2. Imagine, say, an Arab manager working for a multinational firm in one of its overseas facilities in the Middle East. This manager will of course retain his individual personality and will relate very closely to his national culture, while at the same time being influenced in many ways by the corporate culture of this firm. To be effective, this manager will also take into consideration the demands and circumstances of the global markets and the socio-economic-political environments in which this firm operates. National managers who are working with, or for, multinational organizations are able to

Figure 5.2   **Global markets and environments**

adapt to these different cultures; they are multicultural and worldly in their outlook and behavior. Fortunately, during this field research we interviewed many who have worked, or are still working, for multinational companies. Moreover, we have found that Lebanese executives, who were born and raised in one culture, were able to successfully adapt their leadership styles and behavior when they moved to new contexts and new host cultures. For a detailed discussion of this contextual leadership phenomenon, see Appendix C.

Finally, observing the world from a macro-level, we see that it is becoming more economically integrated. However, at the same time, individuals, groups, and societies still retain their distinctive identities and culture. Globalization, an increasingly misunderstood and over-used concept, is not likely to erase cultural differences in the same way that it is unlikely to reduce differences in the political, administrative, economic, and geographic features of a country. Nor is it likely to erase similarities and differences at the individual level. Having lived and worked in the US for a long period of time, we can now see great cultural and lifestyle differences even between each of the four mainland time zones; between the southern and northern regions of the US; and also between the coastal and inland/interior parts of California, where one of the authors currently resides. The same is true when one compares different parts of Europe or regional parts of other continents and countries around the world.

In summary, being culturally sensitive means appreciating other cultures, acknowledging individual differences and similarities, and being able to work effectively with people from diverse cultures. When all is said and done, we believe that bridging cultures and being culturally sensitive are not only beneficial for doing business worldwide, but are also satisfying and enriching personal experiences.

Note

1. For example, does it really matter if the Minister of Foreign Trade of a certain country wears a veil (*hijab* or *'abaya*), a business suit, or a Western dress, as long as she delivers the results?

6
Learning to Lead: Cultivating Emotional Intelligence

Leadership and learning are indispensable.
—John F. Kennedy

Almost as old as the nature–nurture debate is that over whether leaders are born or made. Everything I learn about leadership makes me more than certain that people can be taught the competencies of leadership. At the same time, it is obvious that some individuals have attributes, such as empathy or a superior ability to communicate, that make it more likely they will become leaders.
—Warren Bennis

Earlier in the book we identified five paths to leadership success (Figure 3.1). Chapter 5 discussed four of these paths, namely: working hard and smart; training and career development; personal development; and cultural sensitivity. The fifth path responsible for the making of outstanding leaders is cultivating emotional intelligence (EI)—the theme of this chapter.

This chapter explores how EI drives performance and contributes to organizational success. We begin with an overview of the significance of emotions, followed by a synthesis of definitions of key terms used later on. Based on our field research, we then offer an analysis of the EI competencies primarily responsible for the success of the organizational leader in the Middle East, and how these competencies link with the basic ingredients for success. We will weave in appropriate suggestions for developing EI competencies, which we believe can be cultivated in order to expedite the journey to leadership success. Throughout the chapter we will discuss the relationship of culture to the EI competencies that were ranked highest by our leaders.

Emotions matter

In their Preface to *Primal Leadership*, Goleman, Boyatzis, and McKee (2002) agree that "the primal job of leadership is emotional." The fundamental task of leaders is "to prime good feeling in those they lead." To David Caruso and Peter Salovey (2004), emotions are quite significant too: the emotion centers of the brain are an integral part of thinking, reasoning and intelligence. In *The Emotionally Intelligent Manager*, Caruso and Salovey outline a four-step process model with emphasis primarily on emotional skills. Emotionally intelligent managers need to:

(1) Identify emotions by becoming aware of them and expressing them well,
(2) Use emotions and match them to the task because how we feel influences how we think,
(3) Understand emotions by finding out what they mean, and
(4) Manage emotions, which require us to stay open to emotions and integrate them into thinking.

But emotionally intelligent leaders need to do more than integrate their emotions into thinking. Kouzes and Posner (1995) point out that "leadership is an affair of the heart, not of the head." One of the significant practices of exemplary leaders is "to encourage the heart." When we encourage the heart, we give love: "It's hard to imagine leaders getting up day after day, putting in the long hours and hard work it takes to get extraordinary things done, without having their hearts in it."

As quoted by Kouzes and Posner, love is indeed the secret to success of the US Army Major General John H. Stanford who, when asked how he would go about developing leaders, replied:

> When anyone asks me that question, I tell them I have the secret to success in life. The secret to success is to stay in love. Staying in love gives you the fire to really ignite other people, to see inside

other people, to have a greater desire to get things done than other people ... I don't know any other fire, any other thing that is more exhilarating and is more positive a feeling than love.

Emotions do matter. In *The Greatness Guide*, Robin Sharma (2006) cites Kevin Roberts, the CEO of Saatchi and Saatchi who writes in his book, *Lovemarks: The Future beyond Brands:*

In my 35 years in business I have always trusted my emotions. I have always believed that by touching emotion you get the best people to work with you, the best clients to inspire you, the best partners and most devoted customers.

Roberts then quotes neurologist Donald Calne: "The essential difference between emotion and reason is that emotion leads to action while reason leads to conclusion." In this context, Sharma, Roberts and Calne make an important point: human beings move when their emotions are moved.

The concept of competence and competency

To establish a common understanding of what "competence" and "competency" mean, we will now move into a discussion of EI in general and EI competencies in particular—another of the critical paths on the journey to leadership success.

One of the founders of the competency movement in psychology, David McClelland (1973) argued years ago that academic aptitude and grades were not the only predictors of job performance and success in life. Rather, the success of an individual is better predicted and measured by observing how he or she behaves performing a real job in open-ended real life situations.

Also credited for popularizing the terms "competence" and "competency" is Richard Boyatzis. Boyatzis (1982) defines competency as "an underlying characteristic of a person in that it may be a motive, trait, skill, aspect of one's self-image or social role, or a body of knowledge which he or she uses." Through this definition, a competency represents ability, what a person can do. According to Boyatzis, "there is evidence that indicates that possession of the characteristic precedes and leads to effective and/or superior performance in a certain job."

Building on Boyatzis' definition, Spencer and Spencer (1993) devote one whole chapter in *Competence at Work* to elaborate on competencies. They list five types of competency characteristics:

- *Motives* drive and cause action. The competency of achievement-motivation drives people to set challenging goals.
- *Traits* include physical characteristics and consistent responses to situations or information. Emotional self-control is an example.
- *Self-Concept* covers a person's attitudes, values, or self-image. Self-confidence is a manifestation of one's self-concept.
- *Knowledge* refers simply to the information a person has in a specific content area, for example technical knowledge
- *Skill* is the ability to perform a certain task, for example a dentist's physical skill to fill a tooth without damaging a nerve.

Spencer and Spencer conclude their discussion of competency by indicating that knowledge and skill competencies are visible and most easily developed. Self-concept, trait, and motive competencies are deeper, hidden and most difficult to develop. The well-known iceberg metaphor shown in Figure 6.1 illustrates this point clearly. Thus, the tip of the iceberg represents knowledge and skills. Below

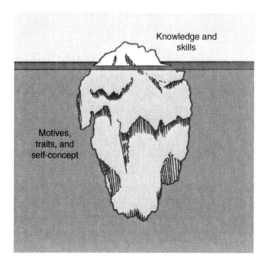

Figure 6.1 The competency iceberg. Artwork by Rima Muna

the water surface are motives, traits, and self-concept making up the largest part of the iceberg; these influence attitudes and subsequent behavior. Attitudes influence "how" a person behaves, and "why" a person behaves in a certain way—attitudes shape how a job is done.

Intelligence, IQ and success

Before we attempt to expound on EI and the competencies of successful leaders associated with it, a brief look at intelligence and IQ (Intelligence Quotient) and how they relate to success is in order.

Psychologist Howard Gardner (1983) identifies seven distinct types of intelligence with respect to talented individuals. The first five are:

1. *Linguistic*: People with this type of intelligence are interested in reading, writing and are good at verbal communication.
2. *Logical*: These individuals are drawn to arithmetic problems and show interest in associations, patterns, and linkages.
3. *Kinesthetic*: Athletes, dancers, and others who are good at crafts process information through bodily sensations.
4. *Spatial*: Individuals who think in images and pictures and enjoy drawing, colors, and daydreaming.
5. *Musical*: Those showing a distinctive awareness of sounds others may miss.

Not only does Gardner's contribution enrich our understanding of intelligence in general, but it also influences a few of the theories and frameworks of EI in particular. It becomes evident from Gardner's classification that no one specific type of intelligence is sufficient for success in life, but rather a varied spectrum with different intelligences. Gardner's multifaceted view of intelligence refutes what he called the IQ way of thinking—"that people are either smart or not, are born that way, that there's nothing much you can do about it, and that tests can tell you if you are one of the smart ones or not. The SAT test for college admissions is based on the notion of a single kind of aptitude that determines your future. This way of thinking permeates society."

Daniel Goleman (1995) explains that Gardner's model of multiple intelligences "pushes way beyond the standard concept of IQ as a single, immutable factor." Such a multifaceted view of intelligence "offers a richer picture of a child's ability and potential for success than the standard IQ." Other factors like cognitive abilities and technical expertise are indeed important drivers of outstanding performance and success. However "our rule of thumb holds that EI (emotional intelligence) contributes 80 to 90 percent of the competencies that distinguish outstanding from average leaders—and sometimes more" (Goleman, Boyatzis and Mckee, 2002).

In addition to these five types of intelligence, the last two in Gardner's taxonomy deal with personal intelligences which underpin Goleman's framework of EI. Gardner summarizes personal intelligences as follows:

6. *Inter*personal intelligence is the ability to understand other people: what motivates them, how they work, how to work cooperatively with them.
7. *Intra*personal intelligence ... is a capacity to form an accurate, veridical model of oneself and to be able to use that model to operate effectively in life.

Having established the significance of emotions, an understanding of the concept of competence and competency, as well as a brief overview of the relationship between intelligence, IQ, and success, we shall now focus on EI and the competencies associated with it.

Emotional intelligence

The management literature is laden with a variety of definitions of EI. We will offer only two definitions by the major proponents of EI. Mayer and Salovey (1997) formulated a concept they called emotional intelligence. They define it as

> the capacity to reason about emotions, and of emotions to enhance thinking. It includes the abilities to accurately perceive emotions, to access and generate emotions so as to assist thought, to understand emotions and emotional knowledge, and to reflectively regulate emotions so as to promote emotional and intellectual growth.

A somewhat less elaborate definition is the one proposed by Daniel Goleman (1995):

> The capacity for recognizing our own feelings and those of others, for motivating ourselves and for managing emotions effectively in ourselves and in others.

Based on this definition, Goleman's framework of EI comprises four domains: self-awareness, self-management, social awareness, and relationship management. Each domain represents a cluster of competencies. In our interviews with successful leaders, we have relied on Goleman's framework and his classification of the 18 competencies in four clusters to determine those that are most critical for the success of the organizational leader in the Middle East.

As outlined in *Primal Leadership*, the first nine competencies relate to the two domains of self-awareness and self-management. They echo Gardner's "intrapersonal" aspect of intelligence.

Self-awareness

- *Emotional self-awareness*: reading one's emotions and recognizing their impact
- *Accurate self-assessment*: knowing one's strengths and limits
- *Self-confidence*: a sound sense of one's self-worth and capabilities

Self-management

- *Emotional self-control*: keeping disruptive emotions and impulses under control
- *Transparency*: displaying honesty, integrity, and trustworthiness
- *Adaptability*: flexibility in adapting to changing situations or overcoming obstacles
- *Achievement*: the drive to improve performance to meet inner standards of excellence
- *Initiative*: readiness to act and seize opportunities
- *Optimism*: seeing the upside in events

The above competencies deal with personal competence (competencies which determine how we manage ourselves). The second set of competencies deals with social competence (how we manage relationships) and includes the other two domains of social awareness and relationship management. These echo Gardner's "interpersonal" intelligence and comprise the following competencies, once again, according to Goleman:

Social awareness

- *Empathy*: sensing others' emotions, understanding their perspective, and taking active interest in their concerns
- *Organizational awareness*: reading the currents, decision networks, and politics at the organizational level
- *Service*: recognizing and meeting follower, client, or customer needs

Relationship management

- *Inspirational leadership*: guiding and motivating with a compelling vision
- *Influence*: wielding a range of tactics for persuasion
- *Developing others*: bolstering others' abilities through feedback and guidance
- *Change catalyst*: initiating, managing, and leading in a new direction
- *Conflict management*: resolving disagreements
- *Teamwork and collaboration*: forging and cementing close relationships

Figure 6.2 simplifies visually Goleman's competency framework with the 18 competencies arranged in clusters and grouped under their corresponding domains.

The four domains interact in an interesting way, and there exists a powerful synergy among them. Successful performance of effective leaders is the result of this interaction: the synergy starts with a successful leader displaying first self-awareness followed by self-management—that is, he or she needs to show personal competence initially. The interaction continues when the other two domains of social awareness and relationship management are at play. Personal competence precedes social competence.

To depict such interaction, we will borrow some specific EI competencies from the four domains. A leader needs first to

Self-awareness	Social awareness
• Emotional self-awareness • Accurate self-assessment • Self-confidence	• Empathy • Organizational awareness • Service orientation
Self-management	**Relationship management**
• Emotional self-control • Transparency • Adaptability • Achievement orientation • Initiative • Optimism	• Developing others • Inspirational leadership • Influence • Change catalyst • Conflict management • Teamwork and collaboration

Figure 6.2   The competency framework

recognize how emotions influence actions (the emotional self-awareness competency in the self-awareness domain). If this individual is unable to recognize self-awareness, he or she may be in a difficult position to exercise sound control over his or her emotions (the competency of emotional self-control in the domain of self-management). Individuals who are better able to control and manage their own emotions are most likely to be better equipped to show, say, empathy (empathy in the social awareness domain) and later to coach and counsel their subordinates or cultivate strong relationships (developing others and teamwork and collaboration—two competencies belonging to relationship management).

Developing mastery in all 18 competencies is presumptuous and would probably take a lifetime. Similarly, trying to come up with a cookbook recipe of leadership success is a daunting task, particularly when we take into consideration cultural differences. However, a few truisms about EI competencies are in order at this point. First, these competencies are not innate talents, but "learned abilities, each of which has a unique contribution to making leaders more resonant [inspiring, engaging and more attuned to people's feelings] and therefore more effective" (Goleman, Boyatzis, and Mckee, 2002).

Second, leaders do not need to master every competency to be successful; some competencies compensate for others, and "highly effective leaders typically exhibit a critical mass of strength in a half dozen or so EI competencies." The authors explain that "there are many paths to excellence, and superb leaders can possess different personal styles. Still we find effective leaders typically demonstrate strengths in at least one competence from each of the four fundamental areas of emotional intelligence."

Third, certain combinations of competencies may contribute to outstanding performance.

So what are the critical EI competencies needed for leadership success according to Goleman? And which of them contribute to outstanding performance? Furthermore, how do the competencies responsible for the success of the organizational leader in the Middle East compare with Goleman's algorithm?

The following illustration highlights Goleman's combination of competencies necessary for success.

The algorithm in Figure 6.3 is the result of research done by Goleman, Boyatzis and the Hay Group. The six competencies displayed in bold type are critical and often displayed by effective leaders. In the self-awareness domain, all three competencies are mandatory. In other domains, some competencies may compensate for a few others, as the brackets indicate. To exhibit strength in the self-management domain, for example, only three competencies are needed: emotional self-control is mandatory, while transparency or adaptability, plus one of the last three competencies (achievement orientation, initiative, or optimism) will suffice.

Strength in a certain competency is measured by behavioral indicators, and overall strength in all four domains may be assessed through the Emotional Competence Inventory (ECI), a multi-rater 360 degree instrument developed by the Hay Acquisition Company.

Our research did not delve into specific measurements of the strength of each and every competency. While we did use all 18 competencies of the Goleman framework in our questionnaire, we resorted to the open-ended interview as a primary tool for data collection. As part of the interview, the 310 successful managers

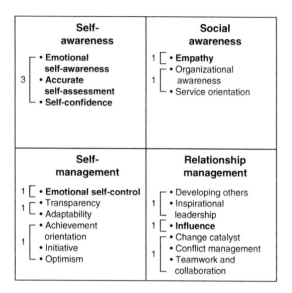

Figure 6.3   The EI competencies algorithm

were asked to rank the importance of all 18 competencies to their success. To facilitate the ranking, the 18 competencies were split into two groups of nine each. The first nine covered the two domains of self-awareness and self-management; the second nine related to social awareness and relationship management. Interviewees were later probed to substantiate their top rankings with real-life examples. Our research findings are presented in the next two sections: one covering the first nine of the 18 competencies, and the second section covering the last nine.

The research findings

The first nine competencies: Self-awareness and self-management

The 310 successful leaders ranked the EI competencies of self-awareness and self-management according to their importance to their success on a ranking scale of 1 to 9 (most to least important to their success). The overall rankings of all nine competencies appear in Table 6.1:

Table 6.1   **Rankings of the first nine competencies**

Ranking	Competencies
1	Accurate self-assessment
2	Self-confidence
3	Adaptability
4	Transparency
5	Achievement orientation
6	Initiative
7	Optimism
8	Emotional self-awareness
9	Emotional self control

Table 6.2   **Summary of the top four ranking competencies**

Ranking	Accurate self-assessment	Self-confidence	Adaptability	Transparency
1	26%	21%	9%	14%
2	15%	17%	16%	12%
3	14%	16%	14%	11%
Subtotal	55%	54%	39%	37%
4–9	45%	46%	61%	63%
Grand Total	100%	100%	100%	100%

Note: Details of the rankings of the first nine competencies are presented in Table A.10.

Table 6.2 reveals the top four ranking competencies of accurate self-assessment (55 percent), self-confidence (54 percent), adaptability (39 percent), and transparency (37 percent).

An analysis of the top-ranking competencies of accurate self-assessment, self-confidence, and transparency follows. As a first ranking competency, transparency was endorsed by 14 percent of the leaders, and adaptability received 9 percent. A discussion of adaptability is delayed until the next chapter because it fits better within the context of leadership behavior and flexibility of leadership styles.

Accurate self-awareness and self-confidence

No one leader sets out to be a leader. People set out to live their lives, expressing themselves fully. When that expression is of value, they become leaders. So the point is to become yourself, to use yourself completely—all your skills, gifts, and energies—in order to make your vision manifest. You must withhold nothing. You, must, in sum, become the person you started out to be, and to enjoy the process of becoming.

Warren Bennis

In an article written by George, Sims, McLean, and Mayer (2007) titled 'Discovering Your Authentic Leadership," the authors describe a critical component that every great leader needs in his or her journey toward authentic leadership. They wrote, "When the 75 members of the Stanford Graduate School of Business's Advisory Council were asked to recommend the most important capability for leaders to develop, their answer was nearly unanimous: self-awareness."

In our study of Middle Eastern leaders, two of the self-awareness competencies were ranked the highest. How do these findings link with the ten ingredients for success and the five paths to success? Well, it is no coincidence that the two competencies of accurate self-assessment and self-confidence ranked highest. Both are manifestations of self-development, which as we saw earlier was the highest ranking of the ten ingredients for success as well (Table 4.4). The high rankings of these competencies are also reflections of personal development, one of the paths critical to leadership success (Figure 3.1, and Chapter 5).

In the Middle East, an often-repeated saying is: "Seek knowledge from the cradle to the grave." Here is another popular adage: "Seek knowledge even if it is in China." During our interviews, we saw this sign at the desks of several executives: "God bless a person who points out my weaknesses." This saying is attributed to Caliph Omar Ibn Al-Khattab, the second Caliph in Islam.

Knowing one's strengths and limits, as well as realizing one's self-worth and capabilities are necessary and related requisites for leadership success. To identify our strengths, Marcus Buckingham (2007) recommends that we pay close attention to how specific activities make us feel. According to Buckingham, our feelings reveal our strengths. But what does strength actually feel like? Buckingham elaborates using the acronym SIGN:

"S is for success,
I is for instinct,

G is for growth, and
N is for Needs.

When you exercise strength, you feel effective (S). Before you do it, you actively look forward to it (I). While you are doing it, you feel inquisitive and focused (G), and after you've done it, you feel fulfilled and authentic (N)."

On the subject of knowing self and identifying strengths, Peter Drucker (1999) suggests we ask a number of questions: What are my strengths? How do I perform? What are my values? And where do I belong? Let us now turn to the actual words of our successful leaders to examine how they expressed their strengths.

Successful leaders in our research substantiated the top rankings of accurate self-assessment and self-confidence in a number of ways. Three themes emerge from a content analysis of their responses. First, some of these leaders thrust themselves in challenging situations undertaking tasks and assuming functions that stretched their capacities:

"I wanted to be given the opportunity to assert myself as a training manager. I was given the chance and I now am wearing two hats: personnel and training."

"I saw an opportunity in this mismanaged company. I knew I could bring a lot through my contacts and knowledge ... I took the challenge and was hired as GM."

"I know I love numbers; therefore, I chose a career that allowed me to use this talent to the maximum."

"Old timers in the oil sector questioned my presence as a female. I persisted and resisted stereotyping and eventually made it through ... I had to overcome the existing company culture not allowing women to visit offshore places ... I know a lot of challenges are lined up for me, but I'm confident I'll overcome all of them. I know my abilities."

The second theme revolves around these leaders being keenly aware of their limitations and their willingness to work on developing them:

"I know my limitations ... I revert to my manager for advice ... I do appreciate the comments of my boss."

"I had the opportunity to take the position of my boss but I declined—I knew my limitations ... This helped me realize my improvement areas. I preferred to take my time and wait for future promotions. I was not afraid of the promotion, but I was honest with myself."

"I am also aware that by nature I am an introvert person. I tend to be shy most of the time. I am not comfortable in front of people. I always volunteer to speak in public to strengthen this skill in me."

"I am put in situations that are defining moments. I was given a task to give a presentation to a VIP client in front of top management on a subject I wasn't good at ... I succeeded ... It changed the way they thought of me."

Finally, the third category of responses clearly indicates the readiness of the successful leader to invite and accept feedback:

"No body knows himself more than himself. The Arab culture is not an explicit culture, unless you get feedback. I try to institutionalize this concept within my team."

"I seize opportunities to get input from my boss on my performance. I try to work on my weaknesses. I try to constructively take these comments seriously. I get feedback from my colleagues as well. How? I did it by asking them for feedback especially during meetings."

"Last Thursday I met with my direct reports. I asked them: What did I do well? What didn't I do so well? What do you expect from me?"

"When recruiting my team, I recruited in areas where I knew they could fill gaps in my abilities. [I] set up a culture of constructive criticism because I know there's a lot I don't know."

"I am too strict sometimes. If a faculty asks for an unplanned day off, I tend to say 'No'. But sometimes, I go to the Dean to get her feedback on the matter, and then look at the pros and cons and their consequences."

Before we wrap up this section on accurate self-assessment and self-confidence, perhaps a few tips about developing these competencies are in order here:

- Self-reflect. Self-reflection is the foundation of knowing yourself. Make time to ponder over your successful (and not so successful) experiences. Determine your strengths, your talents, and your gaps.
- Identify a friend, a confidant, a coach, a mentor to help you discover some of your strengths. Remember, though, you remain the best person who can do this.
- Develop a learning agenda to move you closer to your "ideal self" (where you want to be). Set goals which build on strengths, are compatible with your personal and professional values, and match your learning style.
- Seek frank, honest, and actionable feedback from people you trust.
- Consider ways to rectify lack of skills. The section on personal development in Chapter 5 lists a number of developmental activities to select from. Alternatively, you can surround yourself with talented staff in those skill areas.
- Be prepared to take calculated risks and to learn from your mistakes.

In the final analysis, not only is self-awareness necessary for managing self but also for managing others. In an article titled "What Great Managers Do," Marcus Buckingham (2005) writes that the one quality that sets truly great managers from the rest is discovering and capitalizing on each person's uniqueness. Such discovery has many benefits: it saves time, makes each person accountable and helps people appreciate the particular skills of one another. Buckingham stresses the importance of knowing the uniqueness of each employee:

> Always remember that great managing is about releasing not transformation. It's about constantly tweaking your environment so that the unique contribution, the unique needs, and the unique style of each employee can be given free rein. Your success as a manager will almost entirely depend on your ability to do this.

Another top ranking competency: Transparency

Thirty seven percent of the leaders interviewed for the study selected transparency among the top three EI competencies; 14 percent of them placed it in the first ranking.

What does transparency mean, and what behaviors do transparent leaders display? More important, how do leaders promote a culture of transparency in their organization?

In *Transparency: How Leaders Create a Culture of Candor*, Bennis, Goleman, O'Toole, and Biederman (2008) define transparency broadly as "the degree to which information flows freely within an organization, among managers and employees, and outward to stakeholders." Here is how one of our respondents echoes this definition. He says: "With the 3G technology, one of the things I did was share the knowledge I had and learned about 3G ... I succeeded in putting some programs of 3G together. All this is related to my values of being trustworthy and sharing my knowledge."

Transparent leaders go beyond knowledge sharing. They live their values—another key aspect of transparency. Living one's values interestingly reiterates the second-ranking ingredient for success—ethics and values (see Table 4.4). It is likely that many of the leader's work ethics and values were inculcated by parents, friends and others in his/her early years. It is also very likely, as indicated earlier, that these values cannot be taught later in life. But what are those values characteristic of transparent leaders? And what do these leaders have to say about them?

Content analysis of the interviews reveals the following most frequently recurring values: trust, integrity, honesty, openness, fairness, respect, truthfulness, passion, dignity, and walking the talk. Below are some of the comments made by our respondents in regards to trust and integrity—two prominent and deeply held values by the successful leaders:

"Integrity is my highest value. When I lead (with integrity), I feel trustworthy."

"Trust is the most appreciated value in my work. Success cannot be sustained if we don't have two-way communication. I am the sponsor of trust as a company value."

"Integrity is the most important (value) and, in the long term, will benefit the company most. I do not give false hopes to employees or suppliers. Being truthful generates confidence ... Trust and integrity go hand in hand."

"Integrity and honesty with the customer and your own team are the most important part of the job. When I present a proposal to the customer, I ensure that all aspects of the proposal are communicated, whether good or bad. I never give a wrong impression or information in order to market a product."

Two interesting anecdotes told by leaders in the study related to honesty as a highly cherished value:

"They miscalculated my maternity leave days and gave me more than I deserved, so I couldn't let it pass. I called HR and set the records straight. There are values and ethics with which I like to live in all aspects of business."

"I was put in a position where I was asked to approve something in exchange for money. That was the first time I experienced something like that. From that point on, values and ethics are always part of any decision I make, be it life, personal, or business."

Here are a few recommendations to promote a culture of candor and transparency in the workplace:

- Tell the truth. "Once you develop a reputation for straight talk, people will return the favor" (O'Toole and Bennis, 2009). Encourage, engage, and empower people to tell the truth.
- Act as a role model for ethical behavior; confront unethical behavior.
- Admit making mistakes.
- Listen intently and welcome unpleasant information.
- Reward openness. Candor and transparency become widespread only when leaders make it clear that openness is valued and will be rewarded. "Openness happens when leaders insist on it." (Bennis et al., 2008).
- Show respect.

The research findings

The second nine competencies: Social awareness and relationship management

Under the domains of social awareness and relationship management, the top three competencies were inspirational leadership, teamwork and collaboration, and developing others. Tables 6.3 and 6.4 show these findings. The most interesting finding is

Table 6.3 **Ranking of the second nine competencies**

Ranking	EI competencies
1	Inspirational leadership
2	Team work and collaboration
3	Developing others
4	Organizational awareness
5	Change catalyst
6	Influence
7	Service orientation
8	Empathy
9	Conflict management

Table 6.4 **Summary of the top four ranking competencies**

Ranking	Inspirational leadership	Team work and collaboration	Developing others	Organizational awareness
1	33%	22%	6%	11%
2	17%	16%	16%	10%
3	12%	15%	19%	7%
Subtotal	62%	53%	41%	28%
4–9	38%	47%	59%	72%
Grand Total	100%	100%	100%	100%

Note: Details of the rankings of the second nine competencies are presented in Appendix A.

that Inspirational Leadership (33 percent) and Team Work and Collaboration (22 percent) were ranked highest by a remarkable total of 55 percent of our leaders—another important phenomenon that we will analyze shortly. Empathy, seen as an essential competency by Goleman, was unfortunately ranked eighth. Middle Eastern leaders would be wise to cultivate this competency to enhance their leadership success.

The top two rankings: Inspirational leadership and teamwork and collaboration

Inspirational leadership entails the leader's skills and abilities to articulate a compelling vision and to energize the team into moving toward achieving a shared mission and a common purpose. The inspirational leader ensures there is commitment to the vision and builds a sense of belonging and collegiality among team members.

Above all, the team members need to sense the credibility of the leader, as expressed in the words of one of our interviewees:

> You have to inspire your people when you set a goal for the company. They have to sense your genuineness. You have to put your money where your mouth is. You have to be a role model. You need an inspirational leader to sail the boat and reach your destination as safe as can be.

Other comments revolved around how successful leaders reminded their team members of their vision and mission during annual "town hall meetings," "weekly conference calls," or even in "daily meetings." Leaders would explain the team's tasks in detail and show their people how these tasks "related to the whole picture of the organization."

But compelling visions are never the result of the individual efforts of the inspirational leader alone. Inspirational leaders ensure that members of the team are aligned to their vision. They consult, listen, show empathy, and ask for feedback. The end result is due to the collective effort of the whole team:

"All ideas and solutions come from the team."

"I listen to managers and staff from lower levels and get ideas that can improve the company."

"When asking for work goals, be sure you know their strengths and weaknesses. Put yourself in their shoes and anticipate possible barriers and resolve them before they happen."

"I need my team for their input—even the most junior staff. They have to know what we are doing."

"The manager is not the most knowledgeable ... It is the whole team that will deliver."

"Good ideas could come from anyone ... [Your] subordinates are good reality checks."

"The theme we promoted last year was 'HR for All' ... I organized lunches at offshore locations and organized meetings for everyone to attend. I involved everyone in information sharing."

It becomes evident from the preceding comments that teamwork and collaboration are necessary vehicles to accomplish the organization's vision and mission. With a leader to inspire the team, work becomes more meaningful and rewarding, the vision more compelling, and the team more energized.

Developing others

"My people call me '*Ya Mu'allmi*' which means 'My teacher.' This is humbling and gives me pride" were the words of one of the successful leaders we interviewed. These words readily reflect a cultural truth—a truth characteristic of the Middle Eastern culture and is best summarized by the famous saying in Arabic: "I become a slave to whoever teaches me even one letter." Of course the word "slave" in this context is used figuratively to denote the act of gratitude one experiences when someone offers to be his teacher, trainer, coach or mentor. Learners become "enslaved," so to speak, by the gratitude of their teacher—their "*mu'allim.*"

Developing others is defined by Goleman as "bolstering others' abilities through feedback and guidance." The leader understands the goals, strengths, and abilities of his or her people and offers constructive and timely recommendations for their development. Let us have a look at how leaders in our research went about displaying this task. One leader resorted to workshops: "I conducted a program to allow even the simplest workers to develop skills necessary to implement the demands of the job ... I believe in recognition and assign responsibilities to those who are particularly skilled." Another leader used one-to-one coaching: "I have one-to-one meetings with each of the managers. This started out a long time ago because it proved very helpful." Still another would coach the whole team: "I developed my sales people by showing them how they could change their approach (to sales). This required a lot of coaching."

The competency of developing others reconfirms two paths to leadership success mentioned earlier in the book, namely, training and career development, as well as personal development. The reader is reminded that 30 percent of our interviewees stated that gaining job experience and knowledge was one of the keys to their success (Table 4.3). Respondents also ranked it third from among the ten ingredients for success (Table 4.4). Developing others also corroborates personal development, the third path to leadership success.

A triad comprising an ingredient for success (the knowledge base), two paths to leadership success (training and personal development), together with an EI competency (developing others) is now formed. When these three components interact, the end result is a learning organization that encourages and tolerates mistakes, considers problems as learning opportunities, and allows leadership and learning to flourish and thrive.

The lowest ranking competencies: Emotional self-awareness, emotional self-control and empathy

We took great notice when three of the critical competencies were ranked lowest by the leaders we interviewed. There are, we believe, good reasons for our respondents to rank emotional self-control, emotional self-awareness and empathy the least important. Could this be the influence of culture?

Middle Easterners are often labeled (possibly stereotyped) as emotional by scholars of cross-cultural research. If being emotional is indeed an acceptable and normal behavior in Middle Eastern cultures, then this may partially explain why our respondents ranked these two competencies as less important than, say, self-assessment and self-confidence. The question then becomes this: are Middle Easterners, in general, more emotional? If so, is being emotional an expected and acceptable behavior in their culture?

To find out, we reviewed some of the literature on the subject of emotions as it relates to culture. Research has shown that the intensity of emotions differs from one culture to another. For example, men in Mediterranean countries have been found to more intensely verbalize emotions and display non-verbal expressions than men in countries such as the UK or Scandinavian countries (Scherer and Walbott, 1994). Any visitor to, say, Greece, Italy, or Egypt will witness firsthand this intensity of emotions in public.

We found that there is general agreement among many scholars that Middle Eastern people, along with Latin Americans and Southern Europeans, tend to display more immediacy and warmer relations than other cultures. Two concepts have been used to explain this cultural phenomenon: the immediacy dimension of culture, and the differences between high or low-contact cultures. The immediacy dimension of culture indicates warmth, closeness, and accessibility as opposed to being cold and expressing avoidance and distance. For example, the more "immediate" behaviors are manifested by more smiling, touching, closer distances, and more vocal animation.

Andersen and his co-authors (2004) wrote, "Cultures that display considerable interpersonal closeness or immediacy are labeled 'high-contact cultures' because people in these countries stand closer, touch more, and prefer more sensory stimulation than do people in lower-contact cultures." South Americans, southern and eastern Europeans and Arabs belong to high-contact cultures. Asians and northern Europeans belong to low-contact cultures. Australians and North Americans are moderate in their cultural contact level. According to Andersen and co-authors, "In countries of the northern hemisphere, several studies have found that southerners within each country are much more immediate and expressive that northerners in the same country." Andersen et al. go on to say that: "Most high-contact cultures are located in warmer countries, close to the equator. Low-contact cultures are generally located in cooler climates at high latitudes ... Evidently, cultures in cooler societies tend to be more task-oriented and interpersonally 'cool,' whereas cultures in warmer climates tend to be more interpersonally oriented and interpersonally 'warm.'"

More important, there seems to be growing evidence suggesting that EI competencies do differ in their importance and ranking across cultures (Ghorbani et al., 2002). Several chapters in *Emotional Intelligence: The Theoretical and Cultural Perspectives* discuss the effects of culture on EI. One chapter in particular, titled "Emotions and the Ability Model of Emotional Intelligence" by D. Caruso (2008), makes a clear point that emotions and expression of emotions are culture-bound.

Another recent study of Italian managers and leaders show that effective executives were more distinguished in the following competencies: networking, oral communication, persuasiveness, and self-confidence (Boyatzis and Ratti, 2009). Perhaps is it a true indication that awareness and control of emotions, as well as empathy, are indeed less important than self-confidence, self-awareness, adaptability and other competencies, which may well be genuinely more important to the success of the Middle Eastern leader.

It is also worth noting that during the course of interviewing leaders, the authors noticed that many of them would study the nine competencies and would immediately say: "But all of the nine are important!" Yet, when they were asked to rank them from one to nine, they ranked emotional self-awareness, emotional self-control, and empathy least important. Could the lower rankings be explained by the possibility that the respondents knew that they are "culturally emotional" (emotional self-awareness); and that their behavior is widely acceptable? Or that hiding or controlling emotions are not the cultural norms (emotional self-control)? We believe that these are partial explanations, and that further research into this phenomenon is definitely needed. Our own research findings are among the first on EI competencies from a Middle Eastern cultural perspective.

In summary, our research findings confirm that cultivating EI competencies, the fifth path, enhances the likelihood of success when leaders follow the other four paths to becoming an outstanding leader. Cultivating EI competencies is not easy: it takes practice and commitment, but future benefits are worth the investment, time, and effort. And as we shall see in Chapter 7, cultivating one's competencies will be essential to selecting and using the most effective leadership styles.

EI competencies and their relationship to culture

What impact does regional culture have on leadership success? How do the rankings of EI competencies of the Northern Arab leaders compare with their counterparts in the GCC? Table 6.5 presents a comparison of the rankings of these two groups in the domains of self-awareness and self-management.

Table 6.6 illustrates the rankings of EI competencies in the domains of social awareness and relationship management.

Table 6.5 **Rankings of the first nine competencies by region**

Self-awareness and self-management	Ranking	
	N. Arab	GCC
Accurate self-assessment	1	2
Self-confidence	2	1
Transparency	3	5
Adaptability	4	3
Initiative	5	6
Achievement orientation	6	4
Optimism	7	7
Emotional self-awareness	8	8
Emotional self-control	9	9

Table 6.6 **Rankings of the second nine competencies by region**

Social awareness and relationship management	Ranking	
	N. Arab	GCC
Inspirational leadership	1	2
Team work and collaboration	2	1
Developing others	3	3
Change catalyst	4	5
Influence	5	6
Service orientation	6	8
Organizational awareness	7	4
Empathy	8	7
Conflict management	9	9

It is obvious from these findings that Northern Arab leaders as well as leaders from the GCC display similar preferences toward EI competencies contributing to their success.

Our research findings also indicate that our leaders have a unique profile of EI competencies, which we believe is in keeping with Middle Eastern socio-cultural values and norms. Consider the findings again, this time focusing closely on the two highest-ranked competencies in each of two EI domains: *self-awareness* and *relationship management*. This is how our leaders, collectively, ranked the importance (to their success) of four competencies from a total of 18:

Self-awareness

- *Accurate self-assessment*: I understand my own strengths and limitations and welcome constructive feedback to improve (ranked first by 26 percent of the leaders)
- *Self-confidence*: I am confident and self-assured, and I know my abilities (ranked first by 21 percent)

Adding the responses, a significant number (47 percent) of our respondents said that these two competencies were a good description of them, and that these two competencies were important to their success in life and/or careers. (By the way, the competencies of transparency and adaptability were ranked third and fourth).

Relationship management

- *Inspirational leadership*: Moving people toward a common vision or a shared mission (ranked first by 33 percent of the leaders)
- *Teamwork and collaboration*: Drawing others into active and enthusiastic commitment to the collective effort (ranked first by 22 percent)

Again, a very large number (55 percent) of our respondents selected these two competencies as the most important to their success. (Developing others and organizational awareness ranked third and fourth).

A few brief comments on each of these four EI competencies are in order. Starting with accurate self-assessment, it can be said with near certainty that many leaders in the Middle East remember from their history lessons at school the famous saying by Caliph Omar Ibn Al Khattab, which we mentioned earlier: "God bless a person who points out my weaknesses." Strength and self-confidence are, as in many cultures, attributes of leadership, but especially so in the Middle East where power and hierarchal structures matter in institutions, tribes, families, and organizations; there is a cultural view that encourages the image of leaders as strong and fully in charge (Ali, 2005).

The second domain, social awareness and relationships management, leads us to ask: "what is the role of an executive in the Middle East?" Muna (1980 and 2003) found that Arab executives assume a paternal or "head of the family" or "head of a tribe" role in their own department or in the whole organization. Followers expect leaders to treat them in a familial manner, and a self-fulfilling prophecy is thus set in motion. Muna (2003) wrote: "The employer (manager) feels that he is the head of the family or tribe: he is sometimes expected to provide care, guidance, advice and control in the same way that one would look for such treatment from an elder brother, father or uncle. One of the managers told us 'I give my employees the feeling of belonging to one family ... Many of the employees see me as a father." Another talked about being the 'head of the family' or 'tribe.' Others talked about visiting their employees at home during particularly happy or sad occasions, or in hospitals if they fall ill." In the current research, we heard similar comments from several of the outstanding leaders we interviewed in which they attempt to inspire loyalty, enthusiasm, and teamwork for the good of the organization.

Additionally, research shows a strong preference for a personalized and person-oriented (rather than impersonal and task-oriented) approach to doing business (Muna, 1980; Ali, 2005); this personal approach is sometimes used not only with employees but also with people outside the organization. It is, therefore, no surprise that the competency of teamwork and collaboration was ranked so high by our leaders.

Another competency in keeping with socio-cultural norms is organizational awareness. As it relates to culture, it is no coincidence that the competency of organizational awareness was among the top ranking competencies. Leaders who exhibit this competency are sensitive to the cultural realities within and outside the organization. They understand the climate and the culture of the organization, as well as its organizational policies. They also rely on a person-oriented approach to understand the forces that shape the actions of clients, customers, and competitors. Such personalized approach allows leaders to accurately read organizational and external realities to detect social networks.

As mentioned earlier, there seems to be growing evidence that EI competencies do differ in their importance and ranking across cultures. Recall the study of Italian managers and leaders, which showed that effective executives were more distinguished in the following competencies: networking, oral communication, persuasiveness and self-confidence (Boyatzis and Ratti, 2009). Perhaps it is a true indication that certain EI competencies are indeed *less* important than accurate self-assessment and self-confidence, which may well be genuinely indicative of the success of the Middle Eastern leader. Similarly, inspirational leadership and teamwork and collaboration might work best for Middle Eastern leaders at this juncture of their changing social and economic landscape.

In sum, we believe, like a few others before us, that different times and different contexts (including cultures) call for using different EI competencies. Consider a recent and widely covered event to demonstrate the point, the ascent of President Barack Obama to the US presidency: he called for change, transparency, and collaboration using an inspirational leadership style at a time when the majority of American voters had had enough of what

Warren Bennis called the "lack of transparency," "assumption of unprecedented powers to the detriment of the legislative branch of government," and "lack of candor" that characterized the previous administration (Bennis, 2009). That moment in history, that occasion, called for different competencies and styles. One can find many similar examples from the corporate world where competencies and styles of leaders varied with the context and the situation, especially during major transitions, transformations, mergers, and other periods of change.

Part III

What Outstanding Leaders Do Exceptionally Well

7
Styles of Emotionally Intelligent Leaders

*The leaders who work most effectively, it seems to me,
never say "I."*
*And that's not because they have trained themselves not
to say "I."*
*They don't think "I." They think "we"; they think
"team."*
*They understand their job is to make the team function.
They accept responsibility and don't sidestep it, but
"we" gets the credit....*
*This is what creates trust, what enables you to get the
task done.*

—Peter F. Drucker

To lead people, walk beside them ...
*As for the best leaders, the people do not notice their
existence.*
The next best, the people honor and praise.
The next, the people fear;
and the next, the people hate ...
When the best leader's work is done the people say,
"We did it ourselves!"

—Lao-Tzu

One of the first things that an effective leader must do exceptionally
well, we believe, is to use the appropriate leadership style for different
situations. In Chapter 1, we wrote:

There is, however, consensus among academics and practitioners that leadership is highly situational and contextual: the leader who succeeds in one context at one point in time will not necessarily succeed in a different context at the same time, or in the same context at a different time, or in different cultures, or even with a different group of followers.

We also believe, like many others before us, that leadership styles can be taught and learned—but it would not be an easy task unless a leader is convinced that his or her efforts will have a considerable positive impact on the organization's climate and eventually its long-term performance.

Leadership styles

There is a wealth of information in the management literature on leadership behavior and leadership styles. Over the years, many scholars and researchers have used a multitude of approaches trying to understand how leaders behave and the factors influencing their behavior. For instance, there were several contingency and situational theories of leadership styles advocating the employment of different styles, depending on the situation and the maturity levels of employees. Some leaders may be task or people oriented; others may be directive or supportive. Still, while some may choose to direct and coach, others are quite willing to participate and delegate. And the list goes on.

Among the scholars who have enriched our understanding of leadership behavior is Daniel Goleman, one of whose major contributions on styles lies in disclosing a causal link that exists between style and outcome. Using his earlier research on EI, Goleman examined how leadership style influenced organizational climate, which, in turn, affected financial results, such as return on sales, revenue growth, profitability, and efficiency. But what exactly is climate? What are those styles? And finally, which of these styles are most preferred by successful leaders in a Middle Eastern culture? We shall answer these questions in this chapter while weaving in the findings of our field research.

There are two major pieces of research by Goleman. The first is his famous *Harvard Business Review* article "Leadership That Gets

Results" (March–April 2000), and the second is his equally famous book co-authored with Boyatzis and McKee, *Primal Leadership* (2002). We have made use of these sources to explain climate, styles, and the impact of styles on climate.

Climate refers to six key factors that influence an organization's working environment. As outlined in Goleman's article, these factors are: "the degree of *flexibility* employees feel to innovate unencumbered by red tape; their sense of *responsibility* to the organization; the level of *standards* that people set; the sense of accuracy about performance feedback and aptness of *rewards*; the *clarity* people have about mission and values; and finally, the level of *commitment* to a common purpose." Goleman and his co-authors (2002) suggest that the climate of an organization—how people feel about working there—can account for 20 to 30 percent of business performance. They elaborate:

> If climate drives business results, what drives climate? Roughly 50 to 70 per cent of how employees perceive their organization's climate can be traced to the action of one person: the leader. More than anything else, the boss creates the conditions that directly determine people's ability to work well.

Six leadership styles were identified by Goleman et al., each springing from different components of emotional intelligence; and each style with measurable effects on each aspect of climate. The first four styles—visionary, coaching, affiliative, and democratic—create resonance ("a reservoir of positivity that frees the best in people") and have a positive impact on climate, thus boosting performance. The last two—pacesetting and commanding—have a negative impact on climate, but may be applied with caution and under specific conditions or situations. Before we examine the style preferences of the successful leaders we interviewed, here is how each of these styles builds resonance or dissonance according to Goleman:

- *Visionary*: moves people toward shared dreams, as captured by the phrase: "Come with me" (Resonant style: highly positive impact on climate).
- *Coaching*: connects individual wants with the organization's goals, "Try this" (Resonant: positive impact).

- *Affiliative*: creates harmony by connecting people to each other, "People come first" (Resonant: positive impact).
- *Democratic*: values people's inputs and gets commitment through participation, "What do you think?" (Resonant: positive impact).
- *Pacesetting*: meets challenging and exciting goals, "Do as I do, now" (Dissonant: negative impact, but useful under certain conditions).
- *Commanding*: soothes fears by giving clear direction in an emergency, "Do what I tell you" (Dissonant: negative impact, but useful under certain conditions).

The Goleman research delves into a discussion of how each style influences climate, and it describes the situations under which each of the styles is most appropriate. Many studies have shown that the more adaptable a leader is, that is, the more styles a leader can exhibit, the more effective the outcome. Goleman elaborates that the most effective executives use a collection of distinct leadership styles—each in the right measure at just the right time. This is described well by Goleman and his colleagues, using the analogy of playing golf:

> The styles, taken individually, appear to have a direct and unique impact on the working atmosphere of a company, division, or team, and in turn, on its financial performance. And perhaps most important, the research indicates that leaders with the best results do not rely on only one leadership style; they use most of them in a given week—seamlessly and in different measure—depending on the business situation. Imagine the styles, then, as the array of clubs in a golf pro's bag. Over the course of a game, the pro picks and chooses clubs based on the demands of the shot. Sometimes he has to ponder his selection, but usually it is automatic. The pro senses the challenge ahead, swiftly pulls out the right tool, and elegantly puts it to work. That's how high-impact leaders operate, too.

In reality, however, not everybody has all six EI styles in his repertory. When Goleman and his team brought the findings of their research into organizations, the most common responses from leaders were, "But I have only two of those," and "I can't use all those styles. It wouldn't be natural." Research revealed that leaders who are able to master four or more styles, and have the ability to change styles as situations change, often generate superior performance from their people. As mentioned earlier, it is not easy to master and use all six leadership styles: one has to unlearn old habits and be coached on how to learn new behavior. Learning new skills takes time, effort, and perseverance—supported by constructive feedback. Awareness of the benefits of situational styles is an important and necessary step on the journey to leadership success.

According to Goleman (2000), these are the six leadership styles and the conditions most appropriate for using each:

Visionary: when changes require a new vision, or when a clear direction is needed.

Coaching: to help an employee improve or develop long-term strengths.

Affiliative: to heal rifts in a team or to motivate people during stressful circumstances.

Democratic: to build buy-in or consensus, or to get input from valuable employees.

Pacesetting: to get quick results from a highly motivated and competent team.

Commanding: in a crisis, to kick-start a turnaround, or with problem employees.

Incidentally, in his *Harvard Business Review* article Goleman (2000) initially labeled the visionary style as "authoritative" and the commanding style was called "coercive." The authoritative leader was described in that article as a visionary who "motivates people by making clear to them how their work fits into a larger vision for the organization. People who work for such leaders understand that what they do matters and why." We mention this here because Middle Eastern leaders ranked the visionary style highly, as we shall see shortly.

The research findings

We used the six leadership EI styles in our interviews and asked our interviewees to identify their primary style and one backup style. We also asked them to identify the preferred style(s) of their own managers. Primary style is defined as the most frequently used style, and backup style is an auxiliary, occasionally used style. In our study of successful leaders in the Middle East, we have uncovered answers to five basic questions:

1. What are the primary and backup styles of the leaders in the study? How do they compare with Goleman's?
2. What are the preferred style(s) of the managers, as perceived by these leaders?
3. Do outstanding, excellent, and successful leaders differ on leadership styles?
4. What other variables impact a leader's choice of style?
5. Does culture, national or regional, have an impact on style?

The first two questions: What are the primary and backup styles of Middle Eastern leaders and their managers?

Goleman's research revealed that leaders who are able to master four or more EI leadership styles, and have the ability to change styles as situations change, often generate superior performance from their people. With this in mind, we chose to focus on the top *four* styles identified by the leaders interviewed for this book.

Leader's Styles: Let us first examine the top four primary and four backup leadership styles of the leaders we interviewed. Leaders selected the democratic style (37 percent) and visionary style (35 percent) as their primary styles. The coaching style was selected as the third primary style by 11 percent, and the affiliative style was fourth with 9 percent. These four styles accounted for a remarkable 92 percent of the total responses. Three of those leadership styles were also the leaders' backup preferences. Table 7.1 below shows the primary and backup preferences of leaders and their managers.

The four highest-ranking styles of our leaders were styles that have a "positive impact" on climate. It is notable that all six styles were used, but with much less preference for the affiliative (9 percent), pacesetting (5 percent) and commanding (3 percent) styles. Keep in mind that the pacesetting and commanding styles are the only two styles that have a "negative impact" on climate and should be

Table 7.1 The top four primary and backup leadership styles

	Primary	Backup
Leader's style	Democratic–37%	Democratic–26%
	Visionary–35%	Coaching–18%
	Coaching–11%	Visionary–17%
	Affiliative–9%	Commanding–15%
Manager's style	Democratic–36%	Democratic–22%
	Visionary–18%	Coaching–20%
	Commanding–17%	Commanding–19%
	Pacesetting–13%	Pacesetting–16%

used with caution and only occasionally, according to Goleman. Therefore, our research findings are essentially in line with Goleman's research on leadership styles: Middle Eastern leaders use all six styles, and 92 percent of them indicated that they use the four "positive impact" styles significantly more often than the "negative impact" styles.

Manager's style: During our interviews, we asked the leaders to identify the two styles that are most frequently used by their own managers. The manager's top four primary styles, as identified by 84 percent our interviewees, were the democratic style (36 percent), visionary style (18 percent), commanding style (17 percent), and pacesetting (13 percent). The commanding and pacesetting styles were also the managers' third and fourth-ranking backup style and the only "negative impact" styles. The "positive impact" coaching style was the second backup style.

Clearly, the leaders we interviewed felt that their own managers use two "negative impact" styles which they themselves did not use as their primary styles (commanding and pacesetting). However, it should be quickly noted that 36 percent of them said that their managers use the democratic style—a "positive impact" style, while 18 percent of them indicated that their managers use the visionary style. In short, the leaders in our study felt that their own managers are much more autocratic than themselves, an interesting finding which will be covered in more detail when we discuss decision-making styles in the following chapter.

The above findings were corroborated by comments made by the leaders interviewed. Here are what some of them said when asked to cite examples on the four most favored styles—three of which were favored by both the leaders and their managers:

First, let us look at how the *democratic* style was put into practice:

"I always try to put different options in front of my people, and the options are discussed and evaluated. I do this because my people are highly experienced."

"We get everyone involved, be it a major strategic issue, or minor concerns like social events."

"Whenever we pursue a big investment deal, I like to hear the opinion of my guys, what red flags do they see? And I take it from there for the final decision."

"In some instances, tasks have to be done, and I ask for advice and input from my more experienced employees."

"I always try to stimulate my people by asking them how they think."

"We always ask our employees for their feedback, opinions, and suggestions. We want them to feel they are part of the team. We want them to know what's in it for them."

"We have town hall meetings. I gather the top 80 managers to review our vision and our strategy, and I listen."

"I met with the Executive Chef, the F&B Supervisor, explained the mobilization plan and asked for their input. You give them the challenge and the benefit of making a decision. I could have done it by myself and taken credit. We're not here to take credit. We are here to leave a legacy."

"I never work by myself; the overall planning is done always by talking to other people."

"We were looking for a General Manager who will be in charge of 60 individuals. I went to the managers and asked for their selection criteria. They gave me a list of potential candidates, but I was skeptical about one on the list ... I went around, asked others, got more information and made a decision."

Second, preference toward the *visionary* style was expressed in comments like:

"I tell them why we are here. People have to fit, to connect and align with the company objectives."

"I think strategically. I know the needs of the organization. I ask the team: how do we do this?"

"I cannot impose my style. Followers have to believe in their leaders."

"I share my vision and mission with the whole team. I explain to everyone how our mission/vision must shape and influence our objectives and plans. I try to show everyone how the goals of the company affect their personal career goals."

"My people get inspired when they see me achieve results. They start by being skeptical at first, but then they change their perception when they see me leading the change and working hard to make the difference."

Third, the *coaching* style was yet another preference. Enough was said about developing others in Chapter 6, so we will be satisfied with a few quotations here exemplifying the coaching style:

"When we tried blended learning, all were against it first, but I piloted it and asked them to try it out. I asked them what they thought. They were reluctant at first but are happy with it now."

"Last week a clerk was using a certain format of Excel. I suggested an improvement. 'Try this,' I said. She responded well and became more creative."

"Develop the staff. Get them to the point of empowerment. All this is based on targets and needs. Give them the tools, systems, knowledge, skills and confidence."

Finally, these comments illustrate how leaders used the *commanding* style:

"We don't have the luxury to explain things. A competitor gives a 25% discount. I need to act. I simply can't wait for anybody's input."

"When faced with lack of confidence (like losing a Director), you have to interfere to save the situation."

The third question: Do outstanding, excellent, and successful leaders differ on leadership styles?

The third question relating to leadership styles is: do outstanding, excellent, and successful leaders differ on leadership styles?

The first noticeable observation is the impact of the type of the leader's accomplishments on style. The reader recalls that we have categorized executives in this study as *successful, excellent,* or *outstanding* leaders. To recap:

Successful leaders include those successfully carrying out the basic job functions or successfully implementing projects/ideas as suggested or initiated by upper management.

Excellent leaders are those who have exhibited active leadership and participation in significant advances in performance at the individual and group levels (e.g. improvements in productivity or quality of work).

Outstanding leaders are those who have made multiple, highly innovative, and significant contributions to (a) the betterment of national employees; and/or (b) productivity, cost improvement, customer service, or marketing; and/or (c) enhancement of organizational objectives and strategies.

While Middle Eastern leaders belonging to all three categories consistently selected the democratic and visionary styles as primary preferences, it was no surprise that 46 percent of outstanding leaders selected visionary as their primary leadership style. There is wide agreement among practitioners and scholars that great leaders are visionary, and that they lead others with a visionary style. Excellent leaders selected a wider repertory of backup styles including coaching and commanding, as well as democratic and visionary. Tables 7.2a and 7.2b illustrate a summary of the primary and backup styles of outstanding, excellent, and successful leaders.

This wide range of backup styles reconfirms adaptability—a top ranking EI competency. Also, the use of the coaching style validates even more the significance of developing others—another top ranking competency as we have shown earlier in Chapter 6.

Table 7.2a Primary styles of outstanding, excellent, and successful leaders

| | Primary style | | | | | | |
Category	Affiliative	Coaching	Commanding	Democratic	Pace setting	Visionary	Grand total
Outstanding	6%	5%	3%	35%	5%	46%	100%
Excellent	8%	15%	4%	41%	4%	28%	100%
Successful	11%	12%	3%	35%	5%	34%	100%

Note: Chi-square = 11.7, df = 10, not statistically different.

Table 7.2b Backup styles of outstanding, excellent, and successful leaders

| | Backup style | | | | | | |
Category	Affiliative	Coaching	Commanding	Democratic	Pace setting	Visionary	Grand total
Outstanding	15%	9%	9%	29%	15%	23%	100%
Excellent	10%	20%	21%	20%	8%	21%	100%
Successful	10%	21%	14%	29%	15%	11%	100%

Note: Chi-square = 22.3, df = 10, p. = <.01.

The fourth question: What other variables impact the leader's choice of primary style?

Other variables like geographic region, gender, or age did not seem to have any significant bearing on choice of primary style. Leaders from GCC countries as well as Northern Arab leaders, males as well as females, and leaders belonging to different age groups consistently selected the democratic and visionary styles. Tables 7.3a, 7.3b, and 7.3c illustrate these findings.

The fifth question: Does culture, national or regional, have an impact on style?

Cross-cultural studies of leadership styles suggest that national cultures do have an impact on styles. Dickson et al. (2003) and House et al. (2004) describe the beginnings of the decline in the search for universal leadership principles that apply unvaryingly across all cultures and instead describe variations in leadership styles, practices, and preferences. This prompted us to ponder why was the democratic style the highest ranking (primary and backup styles) for both the leaders we interviewed as well as for their own managers. Is it in line with the decision-making styles, which we will discuss at length in Chapter 8? Is the democratic style described by Goleman more similar to a consultative style than it is to decision making through group consensus? And, is the "democratic" style in keeping with Middle Eastern culture?

The answers to these three questions are in the affirmative. In the next chapter, although we will witness a significant drift toward more power sharing in organizational decision-making styles, the styles of top Middle Eastern managers are still somewhat autocratic and consultative. Additionally, we believe that the consultative style of actively soliciting ideas, opinions, and feedback from employees, while retaining the final decision, is indeed closer to what Goleman calls democratic.

If we go back and read the quotations given by our leaders when describing their democratic style, we will notice that the process they are describing is more akin to consultation than to consensus building or group decision making.

Table 7.3a **Primary leadership styles and region**

Region	Affiliative	Coaching	Commanding	Democratic	Pace setting	Visionary	Grand total
N. Arab	5%	9%	3%	33%	7%	43%	100%
GCC	11%	13%	3%	39%	4%	30%	100%

Table 7.3b **Primary leadership styles and gender**

Gender	Affiliative	Coaching	Commanding	Democratic	Pace setting	Visionary	Grand total
Female	10%	12%	2%	38%	2%	36%	100%
Male	9%	11%	3%	37%	5%	35%	100%

Table 7.3c **Primary leadership styles and age**

Age	Affiliative	Coaching	Commanding	Democratic	Pace setting	Visionary	Grand total
20–9	14%	17%	0%	48%	0%	21%	100%
30–9	8%	14%	3%	33%	5%	37%	100%
40–9	9%	9%	1%	37%	5%	38%	100%
50–9	11%	5%	4%	41%	4%	35%	100%
60–70	0%	13%	13%	28%	13%	33%	100%

Here, again, are some examples of what our respondents said to describe their preference for a democratic style:

- "In some instances, tasks have to be done, and I ask for advice and input from my more experienced employees."
- "We have town hall meetings. I gather the top 80 managers to review our vision and our strategy, and I listen."
- "We always ask our employees for their feedback, opinions, and suggestions. We want them to feel they are part of the team. We want them to know what's in it for them."

As we shall see shortly, the consultative style is in keeping with the culture of the Middle East, which is highly influenced by religion, tribalism, and hierarchal power structures where leaders consult their people and proceed to make the final decision. In addition, we believe that the relationship between leaders and followers remains paternalistic and person-oriented. The democratic style represented by the question: "What do you think?" and the visionary style summed up by "Come with me" may have different meanings and connotations in different cultures.

In summary, our research findings illustrate the Middle Eastern leader's overriding preference for the democratic and visionary styles with their "positive impact" on climate. While leaders in the study employed all six styles with varying degrees of preference, the commanding and pacesetting styles, with their "negative impact" on climate, ranked among the lowest preferences. Another observation is the apparent link that exists between the democratic style of leadership and the consultative decision-making style, as we shall further elaborate in the next chapter.

Additionally, emotionally intelligent leaders are known to increase the enthusiasm, motivation, and good moods of their people—factors that lead to positive results and better performance at both the individual and organizational levels. Finally, emotionally intelligent people have been described by Goleman and his co-authors (2002) as "people magnets," people who have the ability to attract talented people. Attracting and developing talented people represent the third task great leaders must do exceptionally well—a critical task that will be addressed in Chapter 9.

8
Decision-Making Styles, Execution, and Accountability

Consult them in affairs of the moment, then, when thou hast taken a decision, put thy trust in God.
—The Holy Quran, III, 159

Many people regard execution as detail work that's beneath the dignity of a business leader. That's wrong. To the contrary, it's the leader's most important job.
—Larry Bossidy

The ancient Romans had a tradition: whenever one of their engineers constructed an arch, as the capstone was hoisted into place, the engineer assumed accountability for his work in the most profound way possible: he stood under the arch.
—Michael Armstrong

Over 40 years ago, Peter Drucker wrote, "Effective executives do not make a great many decisions. They concentrate on what is important ... They know that the most time-consuming step in the process is not making the decision but putting it into effect" (Drucker, 1967). Drucker's words hold true for most executives around the world, although the traditionally slow consensus-building practices of Japanese managers may not agree with the second half of his quote. We can say with conviction that the process of decision making (that is, how and when to decide) is still a critical leadership task. Furthermore, we believe that the decision-making process is greatly influenced not only by the organization's culture, but also by national cultures and their unique contexts.

In this chapter, we examine the decision-making styles of Middle Eastern leaders and the challenges they may experience with execution and performance accountability. We also summarize and integrate, where appropriate, the international literature on these three interrelated tasks—decision making, execution, and accountability—which outstanding leaders must do exceptionally well.

Decision-making styles

Decision making is considered by many to be an essential leadership task. The role of leaders as decision makers has motivated researchers from a variety of disciplines to its study. In this research, we focus on the power-sharing aspects of decision making: how decisions are made, and how much authority and responsibility a leader shares with subordinates. We will examine whether there has been a significant change in power sharing over the past 30 years among the leaders interviewed for this book. The earlier studies by Muna (1980), Meirc (1989), and Muna (2003) have shown that leaders in the Middle East were fairly autocratic in their decision making. The current field research updates these earlier studies, and explores the possible reasons for any changes in decision-making styles.

Clearly, leaders vary their decision-making styles in accordance with the problem or decision at hand (Miner, 2005). Contingency and situational leadership theories (as well as common sense) tell us that decision-making styles depend on at least four main variables: Leader, followers, corporate culture, and the context of the decision.

- The first variable includes a leader's personal attributes such as educational, social, and cultural background; level of experience; and his or her personality type. It includes the leader's inclination toward autocratic or democratic leadership, as well as the leader's confidence and trust in his employees.
- The second variable consists of factors relating to followers: their socio-cultural background; their level of experience and expertise; their maturity; their readiness to assume responsibility;

and whether there is a need to get their commitment to the decision.

- Thirdly, decision making is influenced by corporate culture, which refers to an organization's shared values, structure, systems, and practices; and the overall climate as set by top management.
- Finally, the style used depends on the context of the decision: the nature of the decision; its confidentiality, degree of importance, urgency, and complexity; and whether a multi-disciplinary approach is necessary to make the decision—such as advice or input from other experts in the organization.

Nonetheless, it would seem reasonable to expect that leaders have a natural and preferred style, one which is used in most situations but is more or less adaptable to various decisions or problems.

For the current study, we utilized a power-sharing continuum that has been used by many management researchers in the past (Vroom and Jago, 1988; Vroom, 2000). It is also the same power-sharing continuum that was employed in the three earlier studies mentioned above, allowing us to make direct comparisons with other research findings.

Decision-making style was defined and measured on a four-point equal interval scale reflecting various degrees of power sharing. The four decision-making styles on the continuum are:

Own decision	Consultation	Joint decision	Delegation
Style I	Style II	Style III	Style IV

Style I: The leader usually makes his/her own decisions, but later explains his reasons for making these decisions.

Style II: The leader usually consults with his/her subordinates before making decisions; their opinion may or may not influence his decisions.

Style III: The leader usually meets with subordinates when there is an important decision to be made. Puts the problem before them and invites discussion. Accepts the majority viewpoint as the decision.

Style IV: The leader usually asks his/her subordinates to make decisions, and holds them fully accountable for the outcome of these decisions.

The leaders we interviewed were asked to indicate which of the four styles:

(a) they felt is usually the *most effective*,
(b) they *preferred to work under*, and
(c) they felt their *own manager's style* most closely corresponded to.

Using frequency distribution, Figure 8.1 summarizes the data collected by the current study; it shows the percentage of responses for 310 leaders from 12 countries. The data represent the four decision-making styles of the leaders we interviewed.

A close examination of the data reveals that there are no statistically significant differences in independent variables and decision-making styles (variables such as nationality, age, gender, educational background of leaders; or type and size of organization, and so on; see Interview Questionnaire, Appendix B).

For comparison purposes, we present the decision-making styles by region (six GCC countries and six Northern Arab countries). The results for the "Most Effective" styles are shown in Tables 8.1; the "Most Preferred" styles in Table 8.2, and the "Own Manager's" styles

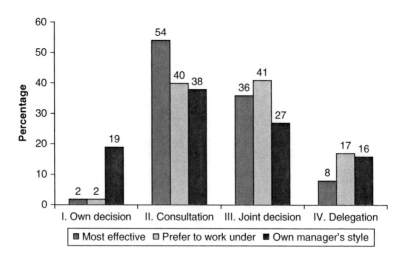

Figure 8.1 **Responses for decision-making styles (2010 Study); (N = 310) (expressed as percentages)**

Table 8.1 "Most Effective" decision-making styles by region; (N = 310) (expressed in percentages)

Region	Style I	Style II	Style III	Style IV	Total
GCC (N = 174)	2	50	38	10	100
Northern Arab (N = 136)	2	58	35	5	100
All 12 countries	2	54	36	8	100

Note: Chi-square = 3.28, df = 3, no significant differences.

Table 8.2 "Prefer to Work Under" decision-making styles by region; (N = 310) (expressed in percentages)

Region	Style I	Style II	Style III	Style IV	Total
GCC (N = 174)	3	39	43	15	100
Northern Arab (N = 136)	1	41	39	19	100
All 12 Countries	2	40	41	17	100

Note: Chi-square = 3.00, df = 3, no significanct differences.

Table 8.3 "Own Manager's" decision-making styles by region; (N = 310) (expressed in percentages)

Region	Style I	Style II	Style III	Style IV	Total
GCC (N = 174)	21	37	28	14	100
Northern Arab (N = 136)	16	40	25	19	100
All 12 Countries	19	38	27	16	100

Note: Chi-square = 2.84, df = 3, no significant differences.

in Table 8.3. Chi-square tests show that there were no statistically significant differences in styles by region; this is a very significant finding that we shall discuss later on in this chapter.

There were no statistically significant differences in "Own Manager's" decision-making styles of successful, excellent, and outstanding leaders, as shown in Table 8.4.

Interestingly, the "own manager's" decision-making styles were almost identical for men and women leaders, see Table 8.5. There was one minor difference: women leaders felt that their own managers delegated more (20 percent) as compared with how men leaders felt (15 percent). This may be explained by the fact that most women in our sample occupied more middle- and more lower-managerial positions, while men leaders represented all three levels, including top positions. Lower- and

Table 8.4 "Own Manager's " decision-making styles (by successful, excellent, and outstanding leaders) (expressed in percentages)

Category	Style I	Style II	Style III	Style IV	Total
Successful (N = 104)	22	35	30	13	100
Excellent (N = 117)	20	39	25	16	100
Outstanding (N = 89)	12	43	25	20	100

Note: Chi-square = 5.48, df = 6, no significant differences.

Table 8.5 Decision-making styles by gender own manager's style (expressed in percentages)

Gender	Style I	Style II	Style III	Style IV	Total
Male (N = 251)	20	39	26	15	100
Female (N = 59)	15	34	31	20	100
Total (N = 310)	19	38	27	16	100

Note: Chi-Square = 2.14, df = 3, no significant differences.

middle-level positions, as expected, are given more authority and more delegation to carry out their responsibilities.

These results are almost similar to the ones obtained when we compared the EI leadership styles of men and women. As we saw in Chapter 7, Table 7.3b, men and women leaders shared their preference for democratic and visionary EI leadership styles.

We interviewed 59 women leaders for the current research, they accounted for 19 percent (59 out of 310) of the total leaders interviewed. See Appendix A for more details. In the 1989 Meirc study, women accounted for only 4 percent of the sample (5 out of 140). Is this progress? Perhaps, but slow considering that 30 years have passed. Lest we forget, women in the West are still facing "gender barriers"—struggling to get equitable compensation or to break the glass ceiling (Vinnicombe and Bank, 2003). However, in the GCC countries, women are making slow but significant progress in entering the workforce. A recent study of the glass ceiling in the UAE, Brazil, Russia, India, and China shows that progress is being made in recruitment and retention of women by multinational organizations, and specially hiring of women in the public sector in the UAE, where "salaries are equal to or higher than private-sector ones, so Emiratis account for less than 1% of private-sector staff but 54% of employees in federal ministries" (Hewlett and Rashid, 2010). Additionally, women have also been recently appointed to high positions in governments. Here are some examples: as of March 2010, UAE has four women in ministerial positions, Oman has four women ministers, Bahrain has two, and Kuwait has one minister. For the first time in the history of Saudi Arabia, a woman was appointed in February 2009 to the cabinet, as deputy education minister. (Qatar was the first in the Gulf area to appoint a woman minister, in 2003).

A significant drift toward power sharing

How do the 2010 results compare with the earlier studies of 1980, 1989, and 2003? It seems that this new generation of leaders differs significantly from the earlier groups of executives when it comes to power sharing. Indeed, there is a significant drift toward more power sharing in decision making. Figure 8.2 shows the drift that took place during the period of 30 years.

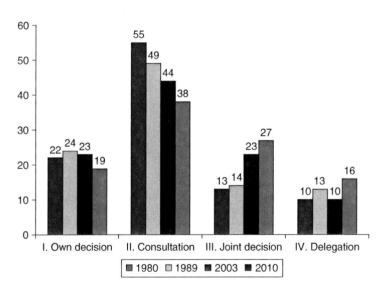

Figure 8.2 "Own Manager's" decision-making styles (1980, 1989, 2003 and 2010) (expressed as percentages)

Table 8.6a "Own Manager's" decision-making styles (1980, 1989, 2003, and 2010) (expressed as percentages)

Study (Year)	Own decision	Consultation	Joint decision	Delegation	Total
	(Autocratic-consultative)		(Participative)		
1980	22	55	13	10	100
1989	24	49	14	13	100
2003	23	44	23	10	100
2010	19	38	27	16	100

By examining the changes that took place in the "Own Manager's" style (Figure 8.2 and, in a tabular form in, Table 8.6a), we see a clear trend toward more power sharing. At a closer look, however, the overall decision-making styles are still skewed toward an autocratic-consultative style. Whether a leader uses Style I (own decision) or Style II (consultation), he or she retains the power to make the decision, and that is what we mean by *autocratic-consultative*. On the other hand, Styles III and IV combined indicate that leaders share their power; we call III and IV combined *participative* decision-making styles.

The autocratic-consultative style has dropped from 77 percent (55 percent plus 22 percent) in 1980, to 73 percent in 1989, to 67 percent in 2003, and now stands at 57 percent: a large, but gradual, drop of 20 percentage points in 30 years. Accordingly, the participative styles III and IV increased from 23 (13 plus 10) percent to 43 percent over that period. To reiterate, power sharing drifted from a frequency distribution of 77–23 percent to 57–43 percent over the past 30 years.

What possible explanations are there for this significant drift? The first thought that comes to mind is that the new generation of leaders participating in the current study were born in the 1960s and 1970s, while the first group who participated in the 1980 study was born in the 1930s and 1940s.

Compared to the older groups, the new digital age generation:

- is more IT-literate (the PC became widely available in the early 1980s)
- was exposed to global media from a young age (CNN and Al Jazeera TV became part of households in the 1990s)

- has wide access to the Internet, Email, and mobile phones (these technological advances became widely used in the last few years of the twentieth century)
- is well-travelled and exposed to other cultures (ease and reduced cost of travel; many of our leaders worked with or were exposed to multinational organizations and expatriates)
- is more educated, well-read, and trained (especially on management topics).

One is tempted to ask: could the proliferation and democratization of information have a significant effect on decision-making styles and power sharing within organizations? We certainly think so. Consider the active role of the youth in the historic events in Tunisia, Egypt and beyond during the Arab Spring of 2011. Highly skilled and educated people (knowledge workers) will continue to seek meaningful work with more open communication and sharing of power.

Additionally, macro-level factors probably had an influence on this gradual drift toward power sharing over the past three decades:

- An overall increase in industrialization and maturity of the organizations and their employees in the Middle East region
- Socio-cultural, economic, and political changes in the region (e.g. in Egypt) and in the world that encourage more involvement and participation (the younger generations are increasingly being asked their opinions by parents at home and teachers at schools)
- Globalization and the growth of international business (WTO and other similar institutions).

Consultative or participative style?

Consultation has a special place in the minds and hearts of Middle Eastern people. It has historical, socio-cultural, and religious roots in that part of the world. Heads of families, clans, and tribes still consult important members before making decisions. The final decision is usually made by the leader who may or may not always adhere to the given advice. In addition, Islam, the dominant religion, actively encourages the use of consultation, which is mentioned in the Holy Quran. In fact, one of the 114 chapters of the Quran is titled *Consultation* (*Shura*). In this chapter, it is revealed that those who conduct their affairs using consultation are considered worthy of mercy and heavenly rewards. Another verse from another chapter of the Quran advocates the use of consultation; see the quote that appears at the beginning of this chapter.

However, when asked "which style you would prefer to work under," 58 percent of the leaders selected Styles III and IV, as shown in Table 8.6b. This high preference for more power sharing has been documented in the past by several researchers (Ali, 2005; Ali and Schaupp, 1992; Yousef, 1998). Yet, 55 percent of the interviewees believed that the autocratic-consultative style (Styles I and II) is the more effective style! And, they described their managers' dominant styles as autocratic-consultative (57 percent).

This discrepancy between the preference to work for Styles III and IV (58 percent) managers and the belief that Styles I and II (55 percent) are the most effective could well be partially explained as a desire to share power with their own managers while they, the respondents themselves, would still use the consultative style II, which they believe was the most effective. In other words, the interviewees clamor to share their managers' decision-making power but would rather be more consultative with their own direct reports. Perhaps this indicates a lower degree of trust in the maturity or in the expertise of their subordinates. Nevertheless, the consultative decision-making style is in keeping with the cultural norms and values of the Middle East.

But consultation must be genuine. A leader who consults but rarely acts on the advice will soon lose credibility or, worse, might be seen as using an old fashioned and ineffective "human relations" ruse meant as a face-saving technique. Non-genuine consultation will not gain commitment, and may well lead to poor execution.

Consultation can be a very effective style when necessary information and expertise are needed, or when guidance is genuinely sought,

Table 8.6b **Autocratic vs. participative styles N = 310 (expressed in percentages)**

	Autocratic-consultative (Styles I & II)	Participative (Styles III & IV)
Most effective	55	45
Prefer (to work under)	42	58
Own manager's	57	43

or when the commitment of the party being consulted is required. And, we believe, that most executive decisions are of that type. Based on extensive field research on the decision-making processes in American organizations, Roberto (2005) concluded that

> Effective leaders welcome others' input and acknowledge they do not have all the answers, but they still remain in charge and retain the right and duty to make the final decision. However, they understand the importance of creating and leading an effective collective dialogue, in which others have a great deal of freedom to engage in a lively and vigorous debate about the issues and problems facing the organization. ... Top executives will demonstrate true decisive leadership when they think carefully about how they want to make tough choices, rather than by simply trying to jump to the right answer. By deciding how to decide, they increase the probability that they will effectively capitalize on the wide variety of capabilities and expertise in their organization and make a sound decision.

Roberto's conclusion is more likely to be accurate in the US where the power distance between manager and subordinate is much narrower than it is in the Middle East. Power distance is one of the five dimensions of culture as described by Hofstede (2001). It refers to the amount of deference and power between people with authority and those who report to them. According to Hofstede (2010), power distance is "the extent to which the less powerful members of organizations and institutions (like the family) accept and expect that power is distributed unequally. This represents inequality (more versus less), but defined from below, not from above. It suggests that a society's level of inequality is endorsed by the followers as much as by the leaders. Power and inequality, of course, are extremely fundamental facts of any society and anybody with some international experience will be aware that 'all societies are unequal, but some are more unequal than others.'"

For instance, an American employee may say to his manager, "Well, Bob, I am not sure I agree with you on this point." This dialogue or conversation is very unlikely to take place with a Middle Eastern subordinate. Even calling one's immediate manager by his first name is not witnessed often. The high power distance in the Middle East would strongly discourage such behavior. Instead, subordinates would address their managers with a more formal, "Mr."; or with the less formal and more endearing "Abu X" (or Father of X). In one of the largest construction companies in the Middle East, the founders of the company were addressed as *"Mu'allim"* (which literally means Teacher), and that tradition is still being practiced today, at all levels of that company.

One of the authors had an eye opener on the cultural dimension of power distance when he was on a training assignment in Japan in the early 1980s. While he was visiting a Japanese manager in his office, the telephone rang and was answered with, *"moshi moshi"*, followed by *"Hai, hai*, etc. ....* " A few minutes later, the phone rang again but this time the manager stood up straight after answering *"moshi moshi,"* and kept bowing deeply and repeatedly as he spoke respectfully with his superior. Even today, one can tell who is senior to whom by the extent of the bow between the younger generations of Japanese managers.

As mentioned in Chapter 1, leadership means having willing followers; and followers from different cultures will have distinct beliefs, values, expectations, aspirations, and motivation—a different mindset. Decision-making and leadership styles will undoubtedly be influenced by the cultural backgrounds of both leaders and followers. In addition to the importance of hierarchy, national culture differences play a significant role in day-to-day behavior such as teamwork, empowerment, attitudes toward time and change, risk or uncertainty avoidance, negotiation, and so on.

In the course of our interviews with Middle Eastern leaders, we found one recurring theme: listening to others, and more specifically listening to followers. Effective leaders had great respect for the opinions of their employees and peers, despite of the centralization of authority and decision making. Nearly half of the interviewees we talked with mentioned listening as a key to success. They said: "Be open-minded, especially to criticism," "listen to others' ideas," "open your heart and listen to people and allow them to open up," "encourage feedback from the lowest ranked people in your organization," "practice the open-door policy," "be an effective communicator," "respect the emotions of your employees," and so forth.

The consultative style (involving a lot of listening along with an open-door policy) was more akin to a personalized and person-oriented and even perhaps a paternalistic style very much in keeping with Middle Eastern culture, rather than that of conventional autocracy (Muna, 1980; Ali, 2005).

Finally, returning to the decision-making styles of Middle Eastern leaders, it is noteworthy that 16 percent of the leaders we interviewed reported that their own managers' style was Style IV (delegation); this is a considerable increase from the 10 percent reported in the 1980 study, or the 13 percent in the 1989 study, or the 10 percent in the 2003 study. This is a healthy trend if one takes into consideration the many benefits of delegation, namely, motivation of subordinates, opportunities for coaching and training subordinates, and better management of time for leaders. In fact, there was a large number of leaders who specifically mentioned "delegation skills" and "empowering and delegating" when asked what skills helped them most in their accomplishments during the last three or four years (see Chapter 4); and when asked what advice they would give younger future leaders many said "don't micro-manage," and "trust your employees and delegate." It would be interesting to see whether this drift toward power sharing will continue. Only future research will tell.

Context and situation do matter

We had our challenges with three of the 12 Middle Eastern countries: Iraq, Palestine, and Lebanon. Iraq and Palestine were not visited because of the ongoing war in one, and the military occupation in the other. Thus, all Iraqis and Palestinians were interviewed where they live and work in the ten remaining countries.

Lebanon was also a challenge because of its civil and regional wars of the past 30 years, which resulted in a recent, major "brain drain" for the country. Thus, for our research study, we interviewed 13 Lebanese executives who are living and working outside their country (who were nominated by their GCC-based organizations), in addition to 18 leaders we interviewed in Lebanon.

However, Lebanon was also a golden opportunity for us to test an interesting and critical hypothesis that was discussed by the authors prior to the start of the interviewing process: would the Lebanese leaders working in Lebanon have significantly different leadership and decision-making styles than their counterparts living and working outside Lebanon? In other words, do leaders who are born and raised in one culture adapt their leadership style to fit different contexts and situations? To start answering these questions, we took a closer look at the responses of the 31 Lebanese leaders on the decision-making portion of the questionnaire. Although the sample numbers are not sufficiently large or equal for comparison purposes, we suspect that the Lebanese adapted their decision-making styles when leading a more diverse and more multicultural workforce typically found in GCC countries. The decision-making styles were more participative than those indicated by their countrymen who were working in Lebanon. Tables 8.7 and 8.8 show the results for the Lebanese leaders. See also Table 8.6a, which shows the data for all 310 Middle Eastern leaders.

Since these findings were based on small sample numbers (13 leaders from GCC countries and 18 from Lebanon), we have subsequently expanded the scope of the research to cover a larger number of Lebanese leaders, in *three* parts of the world. We interviewed 76 leaders, all born and raised in Lebanon, but living and working in Lebanon, GCC countries, and the United States. The research findings will be published in an article titled "Contextual Leadership" (Muna, forthcoming 2012). Large portions of the article, including the tables,

Table 8.7 Autocratic vs. participative styles for Lebanese leaders, working in GCC countries; N = 13 (expressed in percentages)

	Autocratic-consultative (Styles I & II)	Participative (Styles III & IV)
Most effective	54	46
Prefer (to work under)	39	61
Own manager's	46	54

Table 8.8 Autocratic vs. participative styles for Lebanese leaders, working in Lebanon; N = 18 (expressed in percentages)

	Autocratic-consultative (Styles I & II)	Participative (Styles III & IV)
Most effective	61	39
Prefer (to work under)	67	33
Own manager's	68	32

are reproduced in Appendix C (pages 199–215). The data from this extended study confirm that context, situation, and culture do matter. Successful Lebanese leaders did indeed adapt their styles to the new host cultures. They learned to adapt not only to the new cultures and styles of their organizations, but also to the values and norms of their followers. In brief, they became multicultural leaders.

Execution

Ever since Bossidy and Charan (2002) wrote their bestseller, *Execution: The Discipline of Getting Things Done,* a number of books and articles have highlighted the importance of building execution into both operational planning and strategy formulation. Most of this literature seems to agree that any great plan or strategy is not worth the paper it is written on, if it is poorly executed. Execution is a process—a management process which is often underestimated or taken for granted—that must be linked to decision making and strategy formulation.

It will not be possible here to summarize or review all of the new literature on this critical subject. Instead, we shall cite relevant points from four recent books. We recommend that leaders refer to Bossidy and Charan's book because of its excellent coverage of operational execution, and because it emphasizes people's behavior and organizational change and culture. These authors suggest seven "essential behaviors" that leaders must adopt and sustain.

1. Know your people and your business
2. Insist on realism
3. Set clear goals and priorities
4. Follow through
5. Reward the doers
6. Expand people's capabilities through coaching
7. Know yourself.

Kaplan and Norton (2008) begin their newest book *The Execution Premium* with the following quote, which is attributed to Sun Tzu (the sixth-century BC author of *The Art of War*): "Strategy without tactics is the slowest route to victory. Tactics without strategy is the noise before defeat." Kaplan and Norton write: "Managing strategy differs from managing operations. But both are vital, and need to be integrated."

Then they state that: "A visionary strategy that is not linked to excellent operational and governance processes cannot be implemented."

Their main message is that for strategy to be well executed, organizations must plan the implementation of that strategy using strategy maps and balanced scorecards. "These tools help managers communicate the strategy in both visual and quantitative terms. They facilitate the cascading of strategy to business and functional units and the identification and rationalization of initiatives to execute the strategy."

We believe that Kaplan and Norton's book serves as a valuable reference because of its comprehensive coverage of strategic planning, and for the tools (mainly strategic analysis, strategy maps, and balanced scorecards) and the systematic framework and processes it provides. In short, Kaplan and Norton believe that: "Having a comprehensive and integrated management system can help companies overcome the difficulties and frustration that most of them experience when attempting to implement their strategies—particularly new, transformational strategies." They present a six-stage management system, which they summarize using these words:

- Develop the strategy
- Plan the strategy
- Align organizational units and employees with the strategy
- Plan operations by setting priorities for process management and allocating resources that will deliver the strategy
- Monitor and learn from operations and strategy
- Test and adapt the strategy.

Kaplan and Norton emphasize that leaders must play an active role in strategy execution. They write that "No organization reporting success with the strategy management system had an unengaged or passive leader."

In their book *Blue Ocean Strategy*, Kim and Mauborgne (2005) devote an entire chapter to execution titled "Build Execution into Strategy." They write: "You must create a culture of trust and commitment that motivates people to execute the agreed strategy—not to the letter, but to the spirit." They also advocate three elements for gaining the cooperation and commitment of people involved in the execution of strategy: (1) engagement and involvement; (2) explanation and understanding;

and (3) clarity of expectation, which is built on clarification of standards, responsibility, and consequences. Failure to build trust and commitment, they say, could lead to noncooperation and even sabotage.

Finally, in *The Leadership Code* by Ulrich, Smallwood, and Sweetman (2008) a whole chapter titled "Make Things Happen" is devoted to execution. They state: "Execution without strategy may be blind, but strategy without execution is unfounded hope." They add: "Accountability is at the heart of execution…Accountability means that an individual or team feels personal ownership and responsibility to get something done." It is clear from the above writers that decision making, execution, and accountability are interrelated, and therefore must be integrated and closely coordinated when planning and formulating strategy. It is also clear that involving and engaging managers at all levels early in the process increases the likelihood of success, or at least minimizes foot-dragging or the likelihood of sabotage. Execution requires ownership at all levels of management.

The reader may rightly ask, "How does this fit with the current research on Middle Eastern leaders?" Our research indicates that decision making in the Middle East is still skewed toward an autocratic style. The data show that participative styles (styles III and VI) are used by top and middle managers only 43 percent of the time, as reported by their subordinates. Additionally, and more alarming, we found that 56 percent of our respondents believe that the autocratic styles I and II are usually the most effective styles. One must hasten to add that Style II, Consultation, made up 53 percent of that 56 percent.

This does not bode well for involvement, delegation, or ownership—elements that are deemed necessary for effective execution of plans and strategy; unless consultation is truly genuine and is done at all stages of planning or strategy formation. There is nothing more demotivating, we believe, than being continuously consulted and seeing one's advice continuously disregarded. In other words, as mentioned earlier, consultation just for face-saving purposes will eventually become counterproductive and perhaps perceived as a "joke," as we were reminded by one of the leaders we spoke with.

As mentioned in Chapter 5, outstanding leaders are results-oriented and it is therefore their primary duty to see that every member of the team is carrying out his or her part of the overall organizational plan to ensure the organization's success. Strategic decisions and initiatives often call for major changes and transformations that may impact the practices, structure, or culture of an organization. Invariably this will result in resistance or, worse, sabotage by recalcitrant managers who may see the change as a threat to their authority, power, or comfort zones. Even after a change initiative has been launched, some managers may still lobby for old, familiar methods or try to disrupt and undermine the planned changes. Therefore, involvement of such recalcitrant managers in the decision-making process is not sufficient; effective leaders and CEOs must learn how to build into the process mechanisms or tactics that can tackle the anticipated hurdles during the execution of major transformations (Miles, 2010). That can happen if execution becomes an integral part of planning and strategy formulation. Execution should also be closely linked to performance management and measurement, and eventually to unambiguous responsibilities and accountability throughout the duration of strategic initiatives. This brings us to the last interrelated topic: performance accountability in organizations.

Accountability

In his book, *Seven Metaphors on Management*, Muna (2003) wrote:

> The question of individual and corporate accountability has been on my mind for many years. I was taught that people should be held accountable for results in their respective areas of authority and responsibility. I was convinced then, as I am now, that success in management (and in life) cannot be fully achieved if accountability is weak or absent. Unfortunately, I believe that more and more people are nowadays playing the 'blame game': ducking personal responsibility, finding excuses, pointing fingers and attributing problems to 'circumstances' or to others—rather than holding themselves accountable for their own behavior, action or inaction, decisions or lack of decisions.

Unfortunately, many reckless decisions and actions have taken place globally and regionally in the past few years, not only by governments but also by a number of corporations and business executives. Consider, for instance, the turmoil caused by recent wars or the devastation caused by the world's worst financial crisis in 80 years: neither one has been followed by clear determinations of accountability.

At the corporate level, there is a need for better corporate governance, more integrity and transparency. A decade ago, Jim Collins (2001) found that great leaders (Level 5, as he called them), "look in the mirror, not out the window, to apportion responsibility for poor results, never blaming other people, external factors, or bad luck." Collins also wrote that great leaders "look out the window, not in the mirror, to apportion credit for the success of the company—to other people, external factors, and good luck."

At the level of departments and employees, there is a need for better performance management and measurement systems.

Performance management: From KPIs to scorecards to dashboards

If organizational leaders wish to assign responsibilities and hold people accountable, then performance management and measurement tools are necessary; tools which are built around clarification of performance standards, clear responsibilities, and unambiguous consequences (both positive and negative). It has been said by many that "what is measured gets done," and, perhaps, gets done well. However, as we shall see at the end of this section, there are several "deadly sins" which must be avoided when measuring performance. Otherwise, execution of business plans and strategy will suffer and a lot of time and effort will be wasted, while not holding managers and employees accountable for their own areas of responsibilities.

Measuring and monitoring factors that influence organizational performance have gained prominence during the past 20 years, but this measurement activity is not a new phenomenon. Business organizations have been measuring performance for millennia, well before the Pharaohs, Phoenicians, and Greeks. They continued to do so during the industrial revolution and are still doing it during the current information revolution. There are, obviously, vast differences between then and now. Currently we measure a wider assortment of metrics, and most of these metrics are forward looking—or leading indicators—rather than historic or lagging indicators. Additionally, we employ powerful information technology to yield much faster results.

A variety of tools and techniques for measuring performance have recently emerged. For instance, there were Key Performance Indicators (KPIs), followed by the Balanced Scorecard, and now we have the Performance Dashboard. Clearly, with such powerful tools for measuring performance, it is critically important to measure the "correct" and most useful indicators. The first step is to decide which factors are actually driving future performance and value creation for a particular organization (there is no one-size-fits-all technique). Secondly, one must measure not only lagging indicators but also those that show future progress toward strategic goals. Thirdly, performance must be continuously monitored throughout the year, across the whole value chain from shareholders to suppliers and, most important, from customers to employees. Well-designed performance management systems can facilitate accountability and ensure that it is being implemented in a more realistic and objective manner.

The Balanced Scorecard, originally created by Kaplan and Norton in 1996, aligns performance measures with strategy using four perspectives: financial, customers, learning and growth, and processes. It is now widely used by a growing number of organizations; some even utilize the technique for measuring and reviewing employees' annual performance. In fact, Huselid and his co-authors (2005) have created a Workforce Scorecard that, together with the Balanced Scorecard, is meant to provide the CEO and top executives with measures of workforce performance as well as leading indicators of employees' performance. They describe the role of HR in their book, *The Workforce Scorecard*, in these words: "Our analyses demonstrate, and our recommendations reflect, that workforce success depends on *shared* responsibility between line managers and HR professionals."

The newest technique for measuring key performance indicators, including HR metrics, is the computerized dashboard. Alexander (2007) is amongst several who have written books on the performance dashboard. Alexander calls his dashboard "Value Performance Framework" and he states that the specific goals of the framework are:

- Maximizing long-term stakeholders value
- Customer satisfaction
- Employees development, employability, and satisfaction.

Clearly, recent attempts to fine-tune the processes of monitoring and measurement of performance are a welcome addition to this important field. Thankfully, today's information and communication technology makes continuous monitoring a much easier task. Once again, though, what concerns us most is making sure that the right metrics are measured. This potential pitfall was discussed by Hammer (2007) in an article titled "The 7 Deadly Sins of Performance Measurement and How to Avoid Them." Hammer concludes that the metrics currently employed by many companies make little or no sense because companies are inclined to use measures that

(1) Will inevitably make the organization and its managers look good;
(2) Are derived or encouraged by provincialism (largely influenced by organizational and departmental silos);
(3) Reflect the managers' own point of view, rather than the customers' view;
(4) Are selected without adequate thought or effort, due to laziness, or due to jumping to conclusions, on the part of the organization and its managers;
(5) Are only a small part of what really matters, thus losing sight of the big picture;
(6) Have dysfunctional consequences on human behavior and organizational performance. According to Hammer, "People will seek to improve a metric they are told is important, especially if they are compensated for it—even if doing so is counterproductive."
(7) Are not taken seriously by managers and leaders who are thus encouraged to find excuses for poor performance or, worse yet, to play blame games.

Hammer goes on to recommend four steps toward what he calls "redemption": (1) measuring the right things; (2) in the right way; (3) in a systematic way; and (4) in a measurement-friendly culture. Meanwhile, in order to create the right organizational culture, Hammer concludes with these telling words: "The challenge is that to do so requires the personal time and engagement of the most senior leaders of the organization; they are the only ones with the stature and the authority to undertake such a deep shift."

Whether one is discussing performance measurement, recruitment, or strategy (and for that matter, almost everything we do in life) one has to beware of the *GIGO* trap (garbage in, garbage out). We reap what we sow. The poet Lord Byron said it more eloquently, almost 200 years ago:

> *The thorns which I have reap'd are of the tree*
> *I planted; they have torn me, and I bleed.*
> *I should have known what fruit would spring from such a seed.*

Box 8.1 An excerpt from an interview with a Gulf entrepreneur

During 2006, Meirc conducted interviews with several Middle Eastern leaders on a variety of subjects. We would like to quote part of an interview with one whose responses were related to this research study.

MEIRC: What are the main points one has to remember in order to be successful in strategic planning?

ENTREPRENEUR: I believe that there are six points to keep in mind especially in this part of the world:

1. Once you have a vision, and after evaluating the opportunities and threats, you must have the perseverance to implement the plans. Strategic planning is important, but you need to implement the plans. There are many businessmen who have great ideas, but they lack the determination and patience to execute and implement.
2. Stay focused on a specific activity or field; losing sight is a common problem.
3. Find a niche or some distinctive advantages that are difficult to imitate; it is not uncommon to see a certain business opening up one day, and then the same type of business started next door a short time later.
4. One has to have a lot of perseverance, patience, and of course financial strength. I know too many businessmen who expect quick results and quick return on their investment; they are usually not successful.

5. If a venture fails, admit your mistake and move on. There are some people who hate to admit mistakes; they feel that doing so is demeaning or damaging to their ego.

6. Finally, hire good caliber people and reward them well. The Holy Quran says: "Hire strong (competent) and trustworthy people." Notice that "competent" comes first, "trustworthy" second. Once again, there are too many small and family companies that hire staff and managers who are well below standard in order to save money, but they will end up with what, in the West, is called GIGO, garbage in, garbage out.

Source: Meirc's *Training Newsletter*, Summer 2006.

9
Recruiting and Developing Talent

My main job was developing talent. I was a gardener providing water and other nourishment to our top 750 people. Of course, I had to pull out some weeds, too.

—Jack Welch

My experience convinced me that identifying and developing people with global attitudes require personal involvement from the top. The CEO has to see himself as the chief developer of talent, no matter how large the company.

—Fred Hassan

Experience is not what happens to a man; it is what a man does with what happens to him.

—Aldous Huxley

Larry Bossidy, former chairman and CEO of AlliedSignal, wrote a short but intriguing article titled "The Job No CEO Should Delegate" (Bossidy, 2001). He was referring to recruiting and developing talent. He wrote:

> I devoted what some people considered an inordinate amount of emotional energy and time—perhaps between 30% and 40% of my day for the first two years—to hiring and developing leaders. That's a huge amount of time for a CEO to devote to any single task. It wasn't easy to hold to that discipline, especially when you

consider that I'd inherited a company whose investors, analysts, suppliers, customers, and top management all cried out for attention. But I knew it was essential. I'm convinced that AlliedSignal's success was due in large part to the amount of time and emotional commitment I devoted to leadership development.

Of course, Bossidy is not alone in his thinking; many of the outstanding leaders we spoke with for our research share his opinion. Great leaders and successful organizations all around the world put people development as one of their key tasks. For example, General Electric (GE), among many others, is one such successful company that "graduated" a large number of executives over the years. More GE alumni, as they are called, have become CEOs of other companies than alumni of any other American company. In Saudi Arabia, Saudi Aramco Oil Company has done the same. Many of Saudi Aramco's managers, some of whom attended our seminars and conferences years ago, went on to become presidents and CEOs of small and large organizations, and one became the country's oil minister. Similar career moves have taken place with most of the major oil and gas companies in the six GCC countries.

In this chapter we focus on the role of top management, and especially the CEO, in the recruitment and development process of talent. Our intention is to convince more leaders to play a much more active role in what is traditionally seen as a Human Resources function. True, the HR function plans, organizes and coordinates recruitment and career development, but the decisions must belong to CEOs and their senior leaders when hiring and grooming new university graduates, or more experienced people for key or top positions. Indeed, for certain positions, the job of hiring should not be delegated by the CEO.

Recruiting talent

What role should the CEO play in the hiring and recruitment process? How does recruitment fit in with the organization's strategy and competitive advantage? We believe that there are at least three good reasons for CEOs to become heavily involved in recruiting and developing talent: First, to ensure that long-range succession planning is a high organizational priority, and that a talent pool is available for the future especially for senior management positions. Great companies around the world have always been very good at hiring and grooming their own people; consider General Electric, Procter & Gamble, Sony, Saudi Aramco, and many more. They all have "bench strength," "talent portfolios," or "talent pools" to utilize when, not if, needed.

Incidentally, this is the case in our small firm, Meirc, which specializes in management training and consulting. It was established in 1958 at a time when training and consulting was unheard of in the Middle East; it survived several regional and civil wars and upheavals; and it was forced to move its headquarters to three different countries. When one of the authors of this book was interviewed in the early 1970s, the statements made by its founder, the late Simon Siksek, still resonate today: "We are recruiting people in their thirties to ensure that some of them will lead the firm twenty or thirty years from now." The founder of Meirc added: "We always make sure that we have competent people in their thirties, forties, and fifties: to avoid having an age or generational gap." This same conservative, but wise, strategy is still being followed to ensure the continuity of this organization for generations to come.

In a brief article titled "Cultivating HR: The Leader as Gardener," Muna (2004) wrote: "I have always been amazed how most owners of small grocery stores work hard at finding emergency replacements and successors for themselves, while some large organizations fail to do that for their managers." Long-range succession planning is a task that no leader worth his salt should delegate or abdicate.

The second good reason for active involvement of the CEO is to ensure that recruiting and developing talent is directed toward creating and sustaining a competitive advantage in line with the organization's strategic goals. We agree with Becker, Huselid, and Beatty (2009) that organizations should put strategy, not people, first. And those organizations should invest heavily not in all jobs, but in the jobs that create wealth and value, and in jobs that contribute to the organization's competitive advantage. Strategic talent is a powerful and sustained competitive advantage, which is not easily copied by competitors. Becker, Huselid, and Beatty thus advocate an emphasis on hiring choice employees, not becoming an employer of choice, and to avoid getting involved in the inefficient "war for talent."

Thirdly, leaders are humans and will invariably have a few shortcomings; nevertheless, it is the great leaders who are brave enough to admit their weaknesses and immediately surround themselves with talent that makes up for those weak areas. Several of the outstanding leaders in our study stated that exact advice in clear words: "surround yourself with good people." Steven Sample, President of the University of Southern California, confirmed this advice years earlier when he wrote in his book *The Contrarian's Guide to Leadership* (2002): "A primary challenge for any leader is to surround himself with people whose skills make up for his own shortcomings. This is much easier said than done, because most leaders are more comfortable being surrounded by people who are similar to the leader himself. In particular, it is seductively easy for an entrenched leader to choose and retain only lieutenants who always agree with him and never seriously resist his initiatives. But the long-term success of any organization demands that the leader *not* surround himself with yes-men and sycophants."

Most leaders we spoke with over the years would agree with this statement: "We want to select and hire people who are the best in their fields." But as we go up the organizational hierarchy and into senior management jobs, this could become more difficult. Why? Talented people may become potential threats, or shining stars, or better leaders than us! Collins (2001) wrote these telling words in his book *Good to Great*:

A great leader sets the standard of building an enduring great company; will settle for nothing less.
   A great leader channels ambition into the company, not the self; sets up successors for even greater success in the next generation.

Great leaders would do well to exhort reluctant or recalcitrant members of the senior management team to actively drive the recruitment and development of talent. In his *Harvard Business Review Classic* article, "What Leaders Really Do", John Kotter (2001) described how great leaders encourage other managers to develop talent; he wrote:

[W]ell-led businesses tend to recognize and reward people who successfully develop leaders. This is rarely done as part of a formal compensation or bonus formula, simply because it is so difficult to measure such achievements with precision. But it does become a factor in decisions about promotion, especially to the most senior levels, and that seems to make a big difference. When told that future promotions will depend to some degree on their ability to nurture leaders, even people who say that leadership cannot be developed somehow find ways to do it.

Some hints on recruiting external talent

"Hiring Gets a Failing Grade" is the title of a section in a recent *Harvard Business Review* article by Fernandez-Araoz and his colleagues (2009). Describing their survey findings, the authors wrote: "[W]e found hiring practices to be disturbingly vague: Respondents relied heavily on subjective personal preferences or on largely unquestioned organizational traditions, often based on false assumptions." They added: "Fully half the companies relied primarily on the hiring manager's gut feel, selecting a candidate believed to have 'what it takes' to be successful in any job. What's more, we found that companies based their hiring decisions mainly on interview performance, paying relatively little attention to careful reference checks." The authors summed up their findings:

> It's one thing to take a poor approach to hiring. But what really stuns us is that many CEOs do not recognize their recruiting situation for what it is; some are even ignorant of their company's own demographic projections mandating aggressive hiring to replace soon-to-be retiring managers. Even those who recognize the looming shortage of talent are ill-prepared to fill it.

There are literally thousands of books, articles, and training material on the subjects of recruitment and interviewing techniques. Therefore, we will not dwell on this topic but would like to add a few helpful hints:

- Never rely on the interview alone, and never on one interviewer. At least three interviewers should be involved including the direct manager, and the CEO for leadership positions. Interview and dine! Interview again the next morning.
- Check references and more references—not just the references provided by the candidate, which in most cases are not valuable. Make "source calls" with previous employers after getting permission from the candidate. Ask: "Can we speak with people or your bosses

from your previous employers?" References should include a boss, a peer and a subordinate. Bossidy (2001) wrote: "With outside candidates, it's essential to talk directly to references. ... And I don't talk to just one reference and leave the rest to HR; I try to talk with two or three—even when it feels like there's absolutely no time to spare. ... Many CEOs told me that my reference calls were different from most because of how much I focus on the candidate's energy, implementation, and accomplishment: how does she set priorities? How is he at including people in decision making? Those types of questions get at the real potential of each candidate."

- Take off the masks. During the interview one must probe, probe, and probe—and listen well. Many candidates are playing a role, like actors. The interviewer's job is to take off the masks one by one to reveal the real person. For instance, when asking about past accomplishments, probe to be certain that the accomplishments were indeed done by the candidate, and that they are not exaggerated. According to Jack Welch (2005), the key to hiring is: "Listen closely. Get in the candidate's skin. Why a person has left a job or jobs tells you more about them than almost any other piece of data." In brief, taking off the masks takes time—a very good reason not to hastily rely on first impressions or gut feelings.
- Interview questions should be based on competencies (core and technical) required for both current and future positions. The competency iceberg (Figure 6.1) is made up of knowledge and skills (above the water level), but keep in mind that the most important motives, traits, and attitudes are hidden deep below the water. Use behavioral event questions where candidates are asked to describe actual, not hypothetical, events. Remember, that "conventional" questions, and the answers to these questions, are well known to most candidates—and can be found on several websites on the Internet!
- Verify educational information: a quick call to universities (registrar) to verify degrees is essential when there is any doubt about a candidate's educational background. In addition, we all know of dubious "universities and "degrees" that can be purchased. In short, beware of forged documents or degrees or suspicious qualifications.
- Ask candidates for their compensation history, and whenever possible verify the information and question the components of unusual compensation packages or trends.

- Use assessment centers techniques, especially for fresh university graduates who do not usually have a career track record yet.
- Use the appropriate psychometric tests, but watch out for cultural biases. These tests can be inconclusive and can be passed with flying colors by candidates who know how to beat the system. Here again, there are websites that teach job candidates how to pass these tests!

Finally, we urge our reader to take into consideration the findings of this research when recruiting talent. First, one must differentiate between what we called "potential leaders" and those we called "outstanding leaders"—those with a proven record of outstanding accomplishments. Each group requires a different approach. Second, our research findings strongly suggest that when recruiting younger "potential leaders," one has to dig deeper to find whether they have some of the ingredients for success. The early years of potential leaders are indicative of future success.

Therefore, when interviewing potential leaders one needs to peel the onion, one layer at a time. Using the metaphor of "Culture as an Onion" (see Figure 5.1), an interviewer must examine all the layers that make up the "whole" candidate. Start with the outer layer, which represents the artifacts and general appearances, and then peel more layers until you uncover the person's values, work ethics, and attitudes. Remember, that most potential leaders in our research were deeply influenced by their early life experiences: find out what were the experiences of your candidates starting with childhood, parents, quality of education, early responsibility, role models, self-development, life's traumatic events, challenging work assignments, accomplishments and failures, and so on. In short, determine whether the candidate has some or most of the ingredients for success, which were described in the earlier chapters.

Developing talent

When thinking about developing talent, one is tempted to immediately think that selecting or recruiting people with leadership potential is the first step. Not so! Strategy, not people, comes first, as mentioned earlier in the chapter. The key positions, the critical competencies, and the talent needed for current and future competitive advantages should become the focus of the CEO and the senior management team. Only then will selection (hiring from within), recruitment (external hiring), and development of talent becomes aligned with the strategic goals of the organization. To recap, the main action areas for recruiting and developing talent are:

- Identification of the critical jobs and positions needed to implement strategy
- Development of replacement and succession plans for managerial positions
- Identification and selection of internal talent
- Recruitment of external potential talent
- Development of talented people
- Recognition and rewards for good results

We shall discuss only the problematic or controversial nuances of developing talent. The emphasis, however, will be on the more difficult task of developing leaders for multicultural and multinational work tasks, projects, or assignments.

Identification of leadership potential

One of the most difficult tasks in management, and especially in HR management, is the identification and assessment of leadership potential, whether for the purpose of internal selection or external recruitment of talent. When identifying potential of existing employees, the task often becomes highly subjective, and is often mixed up with the identification of high performance—people who are excellent performers in certain jobs are mistakenly identified as having potential for higher leadership responsibilities. This often leads to the well-known Peter Principle, "In a hierarchy every employee tends to rise to his level of incompetence."

One of our clients, a very large multinational company, identifies potential based on observable and documentable behavior on a number of competencies—clarity of purpose, customer-orientation, or teamwork, for instance. Managers in this company are placed in the "high potential pool" only after two consecutive years of scoring high on the majority of ten competencies, and only if they are also rated as high performers. Thus, one must be "high potential" as well as "high performer" for two years in a row in order to be considered for available promotions.

Of course, identifying leadership potential is not an exact science. If one can discover a scientific measure of potential (such as an X-Ray, a thermometer, or an MRI) one can become extremely wealthy indeed! But the problem is much more complicated than that. One must identify the strengths (and weaknesses) of a leader for a specific position in a specific context. Morgan McCall (2007) reminds us that every strength can be a weakness when the context changes. In a brief paper given at the annual meeting of the Society for Industrial and Organizational Psychology, held in 2007, McCall pointed out the perils of "playing people to their strengths." This simplistic view, he adds, ignores that changing situations call for different new strengths, and that old strengths that served well could become weaknesses. He cites the derailment experiences of several talented and previously successful executives: for instance, Phil Condit of Boeing whose brilliance in engineering was less useful when he became President. Or, Scott McNealy's (of Sun Microsystems) high-minded resolve that began to look like simple-minded obstinacy; or when Carly Fiorina's strengths were overused when no longer needed in the new situation at Hewlett-Packard. Thus, McCall concludes with these profound words:

> Even if we knew which strengths are crucial to leadership across situations, which we don't, and even if there were only one way to be effective, which there isn't, a strength-based approach to development comes short. Development requires consideration of combinations of strengths and weaknesses, giving up some strengths that have served while acquiring new strengths, avoiding turning strengths into weaknesses by overplaying them, developing the ability to use other people's strengths, and attending to flaws (sometimes camouflaged as strengths) that, in combination with certain strengths, can cause derailment. As much as a simpler world of playing to strengths might appeal, when it comes to developing talent neither staying with existing strengths nor simply building on them is sufficient.

Given these difficulties, an organization would do well to assess leadership potential frequently, keeping in mind the specific positions, contexts, and situations. An extreme example would be to identify potential for an executive position with a posting in a different country or culture. The vital questions become: will the potential leader have the necessary technical and managerial competencies required for the job? And, more important, will he or she have the competencies to work across cultural borders or in a different culture? Even then, a certain attribute or behavior that is considered strength in some cultures could be considered a weakness or a disadvantage in another culture (McCall and Hollenbeck, 2002). We have witnessed this phenomenon in the Middle East when high self-confidence of well-meaning expatriates, if not carefully communicated, is seen as "arrogance" or as "superiority complex" by the national hosts. "My way or the highway," for example, would be better accepted if delivered as a suggestion or recommendation from a foreign manager or expert. Similarly, as we observed on several occasions in earlier chapters, leadership styles, EI competencies, communication styles (including non-verbal gestures), and "ways of doing business" do differ from one culture (or context) to another.

The task of assessing and developing talent will become, we believe, more crucial in tomorrow's increasingly semi-globalized world, where interdependence among countries across the globe is continually changing. We will shortly address the important topic of developing multicultural leaders.

Embark on your journey

"One can wait for things to happen to him; or better yet, one can make things happen." This is a wise statement by one of the younger outstanding leaders when we asked him what advice he would give to future leaders. As Peter Drucker pointed out years ago, leaders would have to take charge of their own development process in the twenty-first century. This thinking is true even if one is lucky and works for a great organization that provides developmental activities—being in such an organization is a huge added bonus. Self-development, if encouraged and paid for by the employer, is indeed a great way to start the journey to leadership success. Two of the chapters in this book were devoted to the five paths that can be followed on this journey. Most of these paths require self-development. We urge the reader to follow them, and be persistent (yet, patient) if the organization has the resources and support systems required for developing talent.

Organizations, on the other hand, should start by providing early responsibility and challenging assignments to their young potential leaders. Everyone remembers their first few days and weeks of their career: how early assignments could be highly motivating, exciting, and enriching experiences; or could have the opposite effect as we have witnessed too often with development plans of nationals in some organizations operating in GCC countries. In a few of these organizations, development plans start with the dubious term "Become familiar with ...," followed by a number of lengthy visits to various departments, reading manuals, and socializing with other employees. A frequently heard joke in some companies is "how is our tourist trainee doing?" Unfortunately, these developmental plans are often fixed in length no matter how fast or how well a trainee learns. What can be more demotivating to a young university graduate whose expectations and aspirations are set so low? Or, worse yet, he or she is called "trainee" or "developee" for a number of years (sometimes as long as four years) after joining an organization.

Development plans must be flexible and progress should depend on the ability of the graduate trainee to acquire knowledge and on-the-job experience. Projects and real work assignments should be included early on in the programs, and progress must be evaluated frequently at the end of each phase of a career development plan. Some of our clients in GCC countries have wisely started company-wide mentoring and coaching programs to enhance and support the development of their young graduates.

Developing future multicultural leaders

In a semi-globalized world, more emphasis will be given in the future toward developing multicultural managers and leaders. If a person works for a multinational organization, the opportunities to learn how to work across cultures are relatively easier to come across. Most multinationals provide career development plans that include cross-cultural assignments and opportunities that provide valuable international experience. According to McCall and Hollenbeck (2002), the most important prerequisites for international assignments are the "capacity and willingness to learn from experience."

But, what if one works for an organization that lacks career development programs, or lacks an international outlook? Or, what can one do if he or she did not have an international upbringing or education? Clearly, it is an advantage to have been raised and educated in more than one country. For instance, Dr. Ray Irani is a Lebanese

American who was born and educated in Lebanon, obtained his PhD from the US, and has been leading Occidental Petroleum for the past 20 years; Carlos Ghosn (President and CEO of Renault and Nissan) was born in Brazil of Lebanese parents, was educated in Lebanon and France, and worked in the US, Brazil, Japan, and France. Similarly, Indra Nooyi (Chairman and CEO of PepsiCo) was born and raised in India, was educated in India and the US, and worked in India, Europe, and the US. Or consider Sir Howard Stringer (Chairman and CEO of Sony Corporation) who was born in Wales, obtained his BA and MA in modern history from Oxford University, was awarded the US Army Commendation Medal for meritorious achievements in Vietnam, and moved to the US to work in various positions at CBS for over 30 years, ending as its president from 1988 to 1995.

Incidentally, 52 percent of the leaders we interviewed for this book have studied overseas (mostly in US and UK), some worked for multinational companies in Europe and the US, and some in multinationals operating in the Middle East. Many of them attributed their success partly to these multicultural experiences.

Unfortunately, not all people have these types of opportunities. So, what is to be done? For a start, we believe, a strong desire and motivation to adopt a new attitude toward foreign cultures is required; one that is inquisitive, adventurous, non-judgmental and empathetic. Below are 12 specific suggestions from which you can choose the most feasible and realistic to fit your circumstances, keeping in mind that some of them are not easy to implement or may not be available:

1. Seek positions (managerial) in the international division of a multinational firm, or with a company that has overseas branches and subsidiaries.
2. Request or apply for overseas assignments (not visits) with considerable and specific responsibility for a complete project, preferably working with a multinational staff. While overseas, do not spend time only with your compatriots; go out of your way to mix with other expatriates and locals.
3. Enroll for further education (MBA or shorter Executive Programs) at an overseas institution. Consider London Business School (England), INSEAD or HEC (France), IMD or IMEDE (Switzerland), IESE or ESADE (Spain), Queens or McGill (Canada), to name a few.

These institutions attract executives and young managers from all over the world, and therefore give attendees a golden opportunity to interact in depth socially and academically with people from other cultures.

4. Design a career development plan that includes mentoring by a multicultural leader, or lateral moves to broaden knowledge and experience (vertical career moves do not necessarily develop long-term or worldly skills). Opt for a plan that allows learning from mistakes; learn the skills and roles of your manager(s) in order to become eligible to stand in for them when they go on vacations or business trips.

5. Learn the helicopter view—the skill of seeing the forest for the trees, seeing events in a historical perspective, and understanding their broader cultural context can be learned at any stage in one's life.

6. Play an active role in negotiation sessions with international counterparts, overseas partners, affiliates, suppliers, or customers.

7. Carry out best practice benchmarking assignments in international organizations abroad. Even local benchmarking projects can be valuable in broadening knowledge and getting rid of the NIH (not invented here) syndrome.

8. Make it a habit of reading about foreign cultures, history, and literature or reading translated foreign books. To save time and money, take advantage of the tremendous amount of information available on the Internet.

9. Watch or read international news from a wide spectrum of news agencies. Using the Internet, one can access the latest international news from English speaking countries; for example, try *Reuters* (international edition), *The Economist*, *The Guardian* or British Broadcasting Corporation (BBC), from the UK; CNN, MSNBC, or PBS from the US; and Canadian Broadcasting Corporation (CBC) from Canada. One can also look up the websites of news media in Europe, Asia, Latin America, the Middle East, or whichever part of the world one is interested in.

10. Learn a foreign language; at least at the social conversational level. Watch foreign films (most of these films will have subtitles in your own language). Acquire a taste for foreign cuisine, listen to foreign music, and learn a little about the national sports of other countries.

11. Make a point of taking your annual vacations overseas; including (in addition to touristic destinations) sites and places where you can mix with locals. Make sure to devote time for museums and historic sites in order to appreciate the history and culture of the countries you are visiting.
12. Join, or volunteer to work for, international non-profit organizations or non-governmental organizations (NGOs). There are literally thousands of these organizations worldwide working to feed and educate children, to eradicate diseases, to clear landmines, to protect the environment, to spread peace, and many more humanitarian and charitable activities.

We acknowledge that some of the suggested action plans are ambitious and are not easy to implement. Some require sacrificing considerable time and income (time out for further education, for example)—not to mention family sacrifices and perhaps a new lifestyle. Others may not be available within the organization you are currently with (overseas assignments, for instance). But some of the suggested actions, which may still need time and effort, are within the reach of most people. Wholehearted dedication along with strong motivation and determination are required to accomplish these plans. Finally, if your circumstances do not allow you to do any of the above but you still feel it is a worthy cause for your subordinates or associates, then you can influence their career development plans to ensure they get the exposure and experience to prepare them for future international jobs or assignments.

In Chapter 5, we discussed cultural sensitivity and bridging cultures. To supplement that discussion we present below a summary of seven competencies of global executives that were discovered by McCall and Hollenbeck; we quote from their book *Developing Global Executives: The Lessons of International Experience* (2002):

1. Open-minded and flexible in thought and tactics
2. Cultural interest and sensitivity
3. Able to deal with complexity
4. Resilient, resourceful, optimistic and energetic
5. Honesty and integrity
6. Stable personal life
7. Value-added technical or business skills.

Most of these seven competencies are culture-related skills and attitudes. McCall and Hollenbeck quickly explain this cultural emphasis:

> With our emphasis on crossing cultures in defining global work, it will come as no surprise that in defining competencies, we emphasize the cultural rather than the business dimensions of global jobs. We do not deny a basic skill set that executives need, however. In fact, our executives consistently advised global career aspirants to develop these basic skills as a first priority. ... These competencies are what enable people to live and work in other cultures.

International-career aspirants should be alerted to two more hurdles: culture shock and re-entry transition (repatriation) to their own country. Culture shock is a state of confusion and disorientation, followed by frustration or even depression that results from living in different cultures. Re-entry transition is about relearning the ropes, reconnecting with friends, colleagues, and old networks when an expatriate returns home after an extended period overseas.

Drawing on our own personal and lengthy experiences of living, studying, and working in several countries and continents, we can confidently state that even experienced expatriates will experience varying degrees of culture shock every time they relocate to a new country or culture—even to one that they already know well. The same experience, albeit less severe, will take place when one is returning home to his or her own country.

Culture shock is a normal, natural reaction that should be expected and planned for. Country-specific cultural orientation programs for employees and their spouses seem to decrease the duration and severity of culture shock. Learning to cope with culture shock becomes one more skill and attitude (dare we say competency) to be learned when seeking international jobs. Despite their complexity and risks, cross-cultural careers can be very rewarding and enriching experiences, not only for the executive but also for family members—only if living in another culture is managed well.

In the semi-globalized world of the twenty-first century, more people will be engaged in international careers, tasks, and projects that require them to live overseas or to travel across borders and interface with different people and cultures. If Ghemawat (2010) is right, and we suspect he is, the post-crisis world demands new and more flexible global strategies in the coming decades. The organizational structures and people aspects of these new strategies will require four shifts in priorities. According to Ghemawat:

1. More power will be flowing back to "country managers as companies tone down their attempts to eliminate or exploit cross-border differences and instead look to adapt to local conditions."
2. More US companies will be moving key functions (such as procurement) overseas. More multinational companies will have dual headquarters, one in the West and one in Asia (most likely in China).
3. Organizations will have to become more cosmopolitan and diverse when it comes to "developing a globally representative talent pool."
4. Better exploitation of communication technologies will take place to overcome language barriers and cultural bias.

Gaining multicultural experience is not easy, but it is possible. As mentioned earlier, McCall and Hollenbeck (2002) concluded that gaining international experience is the determining factor for success, and that the most important prerequisites are the capacity and willingness to learn from that experience. It is appropriate to end here by repeating Aldous Huxley's quotation:

> Experience is not what happens to a man;
> it is what a man does with what happens to him.

Part IV

Implications and Recommendations

10
Final Thoughts

School should be like work, and vice versa.
                                                    —Charles Handy

And in the end, it's not the years in your life that count.
It's the life in your years.
                                                    —Abraham Lincoln

As we reflect back and take a helicopter view of our ten-month fieldwork, we find that there were three themes that recurred frequently. We begin this chapter with these themes; later we present the wider implications of the research and offer some recommendations for future research.

Recurring success themes

At the end of each interview we asked the 310 leaders two questions:

- What advice would you give to younger future leaders/managers so they can be more effective or successful?
- Why do you think that some leaders are more successful than others?

People orientation

Content analysis of the answers to these open-ended questions shows that 84 percent of the outstanding leaders believed leadership success can be achieved by being people oriented. Had we asked them to select from a pre-prepared list, we believe that the percentage of people opting for "being people oriented" would have been much higher. Here is how several leaders described this recurring theme of being people centered:

"Listen to your employees."
"Communicate often with your people."
"Take care of your people."
"Be passionate—lead by the heart, not mind."
"Truly understand that people are human beings."
"Develop your people."
"Surround yourself with talented people."
"It is the team that counts."
"Seek and accept criticism from people above, around, and below you."
"Be empathetic with your subordinates."
"Humility, not arrogance."
"Lead your people by example."

Of course, there is nothing new or noteworthy about this list of advice. However, what was remarkable is the frequency of its mention when responding to open-ended questions—by 84 percent of the leaders whom we considered outstanding. The same advice was mentioned by the excellent and successful leaders, but to a lesser extent.

If "people skills" are indeed a critical ingredient for leadership success (a view we share with many other authors), then there are serious implications for how we go about developing future leaders—both in business schools and at work. After all, such people skills not only have to be sharpened, they must also be applied with followers who may well be from different backgrounds and cultures. More important, the application of these "people skills" could vary from one culture to another. Further research is needed to find out the significant variations in "people skills" across cultures and how much of that variation is accounted for by culture.

The spiral of success

Another striking theme that emerged from our interviews with Middle Eastern leaders was the recurrence of what might be termed the "spiral of success." It seems that success led to further success through visibility and an element of self-fulfilling prophecy. Proactive, passionate leaders take on a project or task; they excel, senior management takes notice, the leaders become visible, and this leads to higher expectations, possibly by the leaders themselves and their managers. The psychology of self-fulfilling prophecy induces bolder, riskier, or superior action, leading once again to bigger success and more visibility. The spiral goes on and on.

Should a mistake be made, and if the leader has an enlightened boss, the spiral will spring back to action, albeit more cautious or less bold action. If the leader is not so fortunate with his or her boss, then inaction, indecisiveness, and perhaps lethargy will creep in. Fear of making mistakes or taking risks often has that effect on most people. However, the outstanding leaders we spoke with gave this advice to future leaders. Here are some of the words we heard so often during our interviews:

"Allow your people to learn from both failures and success."
"Learn from your mistakes."
"Don't be afraid to take calculated risks."
"Grab opportunities."
"The more successful leaders are proactive—they make things happen."
"They take bolder and riskier actions."

This kind of advice reminded us of this anecdote: A senior executive committed a costly mistake—his pet project failed, costing his company millions of dollars. When this executive submitted his letter of resignation, the founder of the company refused to accept it, saying something to this effect, "Why would we want to lose you? We have just invested $10 million in developing you." Legend has it that this was said by the founder of IBM, Thomas Watson, Sr.

Farson and Keyes (2002) wrote an article in the *Harvard Business Review* titled "The Failure-Tolerant Leaders," which won the first-place McKinsey Award in 2002:

"The fastest way to succeed," IBM's Thomas Watson, Sr. once said, "is to double your failure rate." [A] business can't develop a breakthrough product or process if it's not willing to encourage risk taking and learn from subsequent mistakes ... Of course, there are failures and there are failures. Some mistakes are lethal – producing and marketing a dysfunctional car tire, for example. At no time can management be casual about issues of health and safety. But encouraging failure doesn't mean abandoning supervision, quality control, or respect for sound practices. Just the opposite. Managing for failure requires executives to be more engaged, not less.

Returning to the spiral of success, we must add that conspicuous success and visibility are usually earned. This requires not only determined effort and drive by the individual, but also an enlightened top management to define, recognize, and celebrate success. These actions motivate the individual leader to do a job well. The story of his or her success travels fast through the organization's grapevine. Positive feedback and encouragement from top management reinforces the desired behavior and sets the spiral of success in motion again.

Life-long learning

Somewhere along their journey to success, great leaders learn to be akin to a sponge—absorbing knowledge, or a radar—detecting change, or a satellite—observing from a distance, and then acting according to the newly-discovered knowledge. Learning to become a great leader requires life-long learning including the most important aspect of learning about your own strengths and weaknesses.

We are told to build on our strengths and surround ourselves with talent to compensate for our weaknesses. That is partly true, but perhaps simplistic. We are more inclined to agree with McCall's more complex analysis (2007), which was quoted in the previous chapter and is repeated here:

Even if we knew which strengths are crucial to leadership across situations, which we don't, and even if there were only one way to be effective, which there isn't, a strength-based approach to development comes short. *Development requires consideration of combinations of strengths and weaknesses*, giving up some strengths that have served while acquiring new strengths, avoiding turning strengths into weaknesses by overplaying them, developing the ability to use other people's strengths, and attending to flaws (sometimes camouflaged as strengths) that, in combination with certain strengths, can cause derailment. As much as a simpler world of playing to strengths might appeal, when it comes to developing talent neither staying with existing strengths nor simply building on them is sufficient (Emphasis added).

Learning from others is another source mentioned by many of the leaders we spoke with. One of the outstanding leaders gave this advice: "To learn, always ask questions ... you will benefit two people, yourself and the one who is answering." At first look, this statement seems obvious, even trite, but consider how GE executives solve problems and make decisions—including identifying who has potential; they ask their young and their mature talent to make presentations to top management. One has to put in a lot of thinking into these presentations—and it is a learning process for the young talent. Or consider GE's Work-Out sessions. Jack Welch (2005), the former chairman and CEO of GE, described one of the benefits of Work-Out by relaying this incident:

A middle-aged appliance worker who was at one Work-Out spoke for thousands of people when he told me, "For twenty-five years, you paid for my hands when you could have had my brains as well—for nothing." At last, because of Work-Out, we were getting both. In fact, I believe Work-Out was responsible for one of the most profound changes in GE during my time there. For the vast majority of employees, the boss-knows-all culture disappeared.

One of the things leaders do well, according to Welch, is to "probe and push with a curiosity that borders on skepticism, making sure their questions are answered with actions." He goes on to state: "When you are a leader, your job is to have all the questions. You have to be incredibly comfortable looking like the dumbest person in the room. Every conversation you have about a decision, a proposal, or a piece of market information has to be filled with you saying, 'What if?' and 'Why not?' and 'How come?'"

Asking questions, of course, is not the only way to learn. Reading widely is another—not only business-related material, but also delving into history, literature, and philosophy. Many of the leaders told us that they were avid readers, as we have discovered earlier in this book. Moreover, self-development was ranked the highest among the ten ingredients for success; as was the case with the "accurate self-assessment" EI competency. Life-long learning, it seems, is motivated as much by curiosity as by a realization that there is always much more to learn and improve—from the cradle to the grave.

Finally, another way to life-long learning (which was a frequently given advice by our leaders) is to "learn from your mistakes" or to "learn from failure." Again, this is not new; Warren Bennis (1989), among many others scholars, has clearly demonstrated the importance of learning from adversity. But to be stated by so many Middle Eastern leaders was remarkable in a society that does not always denounce blaming circumstances or others for mistakes or failure.

Implications

We reconstructed the road map titled "Paths to Leadership Success" (Figure 3.1) in order to focus more closely on the people whose actions, or lack thereof, can impact success. This clarifies the implications of our research for people most responsible for making great leaders; they are listed under the column *Responsibility* shown in Figure 10.1. Every group can conceivably have significant direct or indirect influence on leadership success. The diagram also shows possible actions by these parties at three leadership-development stages, starting from childhood. In addition, we believe that these developmental stages are influenced by cultural, contextual, and situational factors as we have pointed out in various parts of the book.

Leaders: Potential and aspiring leaders

To reiterate, we believe that future leadership success depends, first and foremost, on potential and aspiring leaders. Those who become outstanding are leaders who have self-motivation, determination, endurance and patience, hard work, and a bit of luck (being in the right place at the right time). Thus, if leadership development begins with self, it is clear that the onus is on aspiring leaders to start and continue on the journey to success. The journey starts by knowing one's self, and it continues by following most, if not all, of the paths described in this book, but specifically the five paths discussed in Chapters 5 and 6.

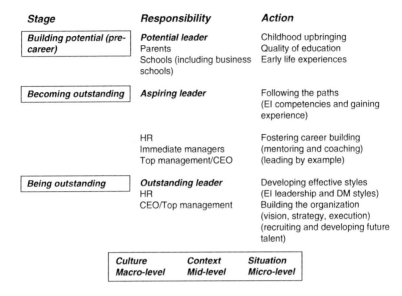

Stage	Responsibility	Action
Building potential (pre-career)	*Potential leader* Parents Schools (including business schools)	Childhood upbringing Quality of education Early life experiences
Becoming outstanding	*Aspiring leader*	Following the paths (EI competencies and gaining experience)
	HR Immediate managers Top management/CEO	Fostering career building (mentoring and coaching) (leading by example)
Being outstanding	*Outstanding leader* HR CEO/Top management	Developing effective styles (EI leadership and DM styles) Building the organization (vision, strategy, execution) (recruiting and developing future talent)

Culture *Macro-level*	*Context* *Mid-level*	*Situation* *Micro-level*

Figure 10.1 The journey to leadership success

Potential and aspiring leaders who work for organizations that do not have effective feedback and performance management systems (preferably not linked to compensation), or formal career development plans should be encouraged and inspired by the wise words of advice contained in the following quotations (some appeared earlier in this book):

- Ancient Greek philosophy: *"Know thyself"*, which is inscribed on the Temple of Apollo in Delphi, Greece.
- Caliph Omar Ibn Al-Khattab: *"God bless a person who points out my weaknesses."*
- Peter Drucker: *"Development is always self-development."*
- Charles Handy: *"The best learning happens in real life with real problems and real people and not in classrooms."*
- Warren Bennis: *"Becoming a leader is not an orderly path. It is fitful, often painful process that involves wrong turns and dead ends before great strides are made."*
- A leader we interviewed for this study: *"Develop yourself; don't wait for the company to do it."*

The implications of this research for leaders who are already outstanding and wish to remain so will be discussed shortly in a separate section. The implications for immediate managers and HR professionals will also be discussed in the same section since all three groups should be engaged in the same three critical tasks. The first task is developing their own appropriate leadership and decision-making styles; secondly, fostering career building of younger or future leaders; and thirdly, building their organization for the future in terms of both strategy and people.

Parents and schools

Parents and schools share the responsibility and the burden of shaping young people. They both have a great impact on each of the top six ingredients for success, which were discussed in Chapter 4 (see Table 4.4). Parents and teachers, we found, can be powerful role models to children and adolescents. In brief, our research indicates that child upbringing and early life experiences are the foundations for future leadership development. Education builds on those foundations. And when one starts a career, most excellent organizations offer golden opportunities to build further on what was learned during childhood and during academic years. Therefore, both parents and schools can benefit by examining the ingredients for success discovered by the current research.

Parents and schools must become cognizant of the nuances of what "quality of education" really means. It means that passing examinations and getting high grades alone are not the sole objective of education. It means that students have to learn creative thinking, not only analytical thinking. Most of the excellent schools know that development of the mind takes place by doing projects and research, not by rote learning and passing exams. It also means that extracurricular activities such as sports, drama, music, art, student associations, and other school activities are essential for the development of leadership and social skills as well as other EI competencies.

As parents we do our very best to help our children get through periodic homework and exams, but some do not seem to realize that spoon feeding will harm more than help the child in the long run. There is profound wisdom in the Chinese proverb, "Give a man a fish, and you feed him for a day; teach a man to fish, and you feed him for a lifetime." In some countries in the Middle East, and possibly many other countries, there seems to be an annual crisis at home and at work: the end-of-the-year examinations period! Parents devote enormous amount of time and energy spoon feeding (stuffing of the mind, as many have called it) to ensure that their children get good final grades. Wise parents, we believe, should put equal emphasis on extracurricular activities.

Given the fact that 44 percent of our respondents held a Masters or higher degrees, many with MBA degrees, we believe that business schools are equally guilty of graduating MBAs who are taught technical and analytical skills, using for the most part "canned" case studies and group discussions. Business ethics, "worldly" thinking, experiential learning, cultural and contextual experience, and even cultural history, literature, and arts seem to be foreign subjects to most MBAs. There have been calls by scholars and academics for major reform at business schools (after the business scandals of the early 2000s, and again before and after the 2008 economic crisis) (Mintzberg, 2004 and Bennis and O'Toole, 2005). Some from academia (Harvard and Yale, for example) even suggested that MBA graduates should adhere to a code of ethics similar to the Hippocratic Oath that medical professionals take, and to revoke the degrees of MBA graduates who break the code (Khurana and Nohria, 2008 and Podolny, 2009a).

Podolny (2009b), the former dean at the Yale School of Management, wrote a commentary in Bennis' recent book suggesting another solution to this controversial subject:

So what is the solution to the problem? I suspect that there are a number of different ones, but I will focus on the solution pursued at Yale. The faculty put in place an interdisciplinary curriculum where the core courses were no longer structured by disciplinary silos, but by the key constituencies or perspectives that a manager needs to change to be effective. So, instead of a course in marketing, they created a course on the customer perspective. Instead of a course on organizational behavior, they put in place a course on the employee perspective, and so on. There are a total of eight perspective courses in the core; each is team taught by faculty from multiple disciplines.

The problem is not limited to business schools, however. For example, many medical professionals, including new graduates whom we spoke with, have disclosed their deep frustration about the lack of basic business education in medical schools. Only few wise students, it seems, opt to take business courses while earning their medical degrees. One young doctor, whom we interviewed by telephone, told us that, after graduating from medical school, she felt that an MBA degree was essential for success in her career and in her future medical practice—a degree which she eventually obtained.

Again, parents and schools share the onus of inculcating self-development, the highest-ranking ingredient for success, as perceived by leaders in this study. Parents can instill the passion for continuous learning early on by encouraging their children to read avidly, refrain from "helping" them complete their homework, and by being role models for life-long learning through engagement in learning experiences such as reading, attending seminars, speaking events, gifting educational toys, watching educational programs on television, and other creative actions that fit the age and situation of their child or adolescent.

Teachers and professors, too, must instill the love of, and the insatiable thirst for, continuous learning—rather than allowing their graduates to believe that they have now "completed" the search for knowledge. We recall how some of us felt upon graduation from high school: we believed that we had learned everything there was to learn; others felt the same upon graduating from university; while most postgraduates realize that even though they have become experts in their specific field, there is yet a lot to learn.

Both parents and teachers instill work ethics, accountability, honesty, and integrity in children and students. It seems that it is a bit too late to do that after one starts a career. The motivational forces that encourage greed, corruption and other illegal behavior, poor work ethics and quality, lack of respect for all stakeholders, and self-serving and short-sighted decisions do not start at the beginning of one's career—these motives are rooted much earlier in life, in childhood and during school years. The leaders in our research ranked ethics as the second highest ingredient for their success. They cited many examples and incidents from their parents and teachers who instilled in them ethical values. Parents, in particular, have a great impact if they impart ethics and values by being good role models; they have many years to teach integrity, honesty, and hard work by example, not only by words.

Finally, early responsibility, ranked as fifth ingredient by our leaders, can begin when a child is able to tidy up his or her room, help with chores around the house, wash the family car, and work part time and during summer holidays. Other tasks that can teach responsibility include volunteer work for charitable or community organizations, preparation of own budgets and keeping track of major expenses during high school and university. We believe that responsibility and accountability cannot be really learned when people are in their twenties or early thirties—it may be too late then.

CEOs, top management, immediate managers, and HR professionals

CEOs, senior management teams, immediate managers, and HR professionals are busy people who are engaged in managing complex organizations. To become great leaders, however, they will have to do three critical long-term tasks exceptionally well:

- Developing their EI competencies, and their leadership and decision-making styles.
- Fostering and building other people's careers by (a) training and developing talented people, (b) actively coaching and mentoring, and (c) leading by example and being good role models to potential and aspiring leaders.
- Building the organization by (a) vision, strategy, and execution, and (b) recruiting and developing multicultural, culturally-sensitive, talent for higher future positions; and simultaneously place more multicultural executives on their boards of directors. Such actions will go a long way to ensure that organizations have the right talent pools for succession planning purposes, and will help them formulate more flexible global strategies.

These three tasks or functions have been examined and discussed thoroughly in the book, and thus there is no need for repetition, except to reemphasize that these tasks impact not only their own effectiveness but the future of younger aspiring leaders.

Human resource professionals (HR)

The implications of our research for HR professionals are enormous. To earn a chair at strategy meetings and to play an effective role in senior management teams, HR professionals should delegate, but not abdicate, more of their responsibilities to their staff in order to devote more time, energy, and thought into the following areas:

- Become more proactive, less administrative and more strategic.
- Link the strategy of HR to the organization's vision, strategy, and its stakeholders. Link people to the vision and strategy of the organization; "Strategy, not people, comes first," as mentioned earlier in the book.
- Introduce and implement succession planning systems, if none exist. Develop the organization's bench strength, and consider both inside and outside talent to fill gaps.
- Identify high-potential employees for key positions (based not only on past performance but also on behavior-observed core and technical competencies. Use 360 degrees feedback systems, if the organizational culture permits).
- Recruit high-potential employees, and start their career development with early and meaningful assignments, projects, and responsibilities.
- Develop people; enhance their career developmental and training activities with formal coaching and mentoring programs, if none exist.
- Introduce country-specific, cross-cultural orientation and awareness training for managers and their spouses before sending them out to occupy positions overseas. Reinforce the training a few months after they settle in the host country through multicultural management skills programs.
- Support the Board of Directors, the CEO, and top management by setting up a performance accountability system, linked to strategy and execution (an often missing link).

Culture, context, and situations do matter

Figure 10.1 shows that the journey to leadership success, with its three stages, is influenced by culture, context, and situation (macro, mid, and micro levels). Throughout, we have argued that these three factors have an impact on leadership success:

- Followers have different values, norms, beliefs, expectations, and behavior—and these differences have to be taken into account by leaders if they wish to lead effectively. You cannot lead a New Yorker or a Texan, for example, in the same manner you would an Iraqi or an Egyptian. A wise leader would adjust his or her styles of communication, interpersonal relations, decision-making and leadership styles according not only to the context and situation, but also culture. Followership and leadership are two faces of the same coin. We discovered, for instance, that certain EI competencies are more important than others depending on culture and context (McCall and Hollenbeck, 2004; Boyatzis and Ratti, 2009). The same is true of decision-making styles. Finally, when working or living across borders, new competencies (for example, cultural sensitivity) play an important role in cross-cultural business management and careers.

- Leaders must take into account the organizational context, too. Certain organizational level issues, challenges, strategies, or problems (and so forth) are unique to each specific organization. For example, there will be important differences in the type of industry, its products and services, the locations of its markets, its competition, its age and maturity, and its stakeholders. HR systems, recruiting and developing people, strategies and execution will have to fit the organizational culture; otherwise, a slower and more painful change process may have to be launched. In short, leadership differs from one context to another.

- Situational leadership, we believe, is still alive. Leaders do adjust their approaches and styles depending on the situation. Emotionally intelligent leaders, we learned, use at least four of the six EI leadership styles for different situations in order to be effective (Goleman, Boyatzis, and McKee, 2002). The same is true when making decisions and solving problems. In organizations, there are many other tasks and functions that require situational approaches and styles, for example, conducting negotiations, sales and marketing, or HR practices.

During the data analysis stage of our research, we looked for any statistically significant differences among the six GCC countries on the independent and dependent variables we measured; we found none. This reconfirms the earlier studies by Muna (1980 and 2003) and Meirc (1989), among others. We also suspected that there might be some statistically significant differences between the GCC countries and the six Northern Arab countries; again, we found none. (For variables, see Appendix A and Appendix B.)

In brief, the 12 Middle Eastern countries in our study are fairly homogeneous on the leadership variables. The best explanation, we believe, is this: although there are vast differences in how people from these two regional areas dress, their cuisine, their music, and their accents, when one starts peeling the onion (Figure 5.1), one finds that the core values, norms, and beliefs are similar. The leadership topics we looked at involve the inner layers of the onion, not the outside ones. The EI competencies, EI leadership styles, and decision-making styles of the leaders we interviewed were in keeping with the Middle Eastern traditions and culture. We suspect the same is true within other cultures but not necessarily so across cultures where differences still matter (Hofstede 2001; Ghemawat, 2007).

Thoughts and recommendations for future research

We chose the title Final Thoughts for this chapter in order to express our personal thinking and opinions, reveal our gut feelings, and share our observations of the world from an organizational behavior perspective without backing them up with "scientific" data. The chapter's title, of course, is not very creative or unique, but it allows us, we hope, to speculate and think out loud in this last section of the book.

Further research into an extremely interesting organizational phenomenon of the first half of the twenty-first century is imperative: a rapid increase in the number of organizations and individuals who will become multicultural, whether by crossing borders, or by staying home while doing business with the rest of the world. Future organizations, large and small, will have more multicultural employees, managers, and leaders, will think and act on a global level, and will become more agile and flexible in an increasingly volatile and unpredictable global marketplace (Ghemawat, 2010).

Ghemawat (2011) states that in today's semi-globalized world, "It's certainly possible to have a global strategy and a global organization in such a world. But they must be based not on the elimination of differences and distances among people, cultures, and places, but on an understanding of them. ... Because denying the existence of differences doesn't make them any easier to deal with." Ghemawat recommends that senior executives should think hard about how to readjust their organizations to better manage cultural differences and distances, and they must cultivate cosmopolitan leaders who know how to bridge cultural and national differences.

Our hypothesis, to be tested by future researchers, is that neither convergence nor divergence in the practices of management is the likely outcome of a shrinking world; rather it will be multicultural patterns, skills, and behavior that will count and will lead to success. To use metaphors: the world is becoming smaller but remains round and will become more competitive, with a colorful mosaic, rather than simply a "flat world."

We agree with Friedman (2005) that the world has shrunk to a smaller size; and this shrinking has been happening for ages and, incidentally, since well before Christopher Columbus embarked on his journey to discover India (the Arabs, for example, bridged the Middle East and Spain many centuries earlier). However, we believe that the world will continue to have many arenas, contours, and walls, some not so flat. Different parts of the world will continue to have colors, feel, flavors, and tastes and odors different from the ones "back home," not to mention differences in the economic, religious, political, and governmental spheres. Yes, technology and software have shrunk the world, but the slower-changing software of the mind and mental programs (that is, culture according to Hofstede) still have significant effects on organizational and individual behavior (Hofstede, 2001).

"Melting pots" and "flat worlds" may turn out to be over-simplification of reality, we think. One needs to live and work for some time in a "melting pot" or a "flat world" to realize that differences in culture are persistent and still exist. A short-term visitor living in comfortable hotels may think otherwise, but not so for a person who is immersed in these contexts and who will invariably experience culture shock after a few months of living overseas. One needs to keep peeling the proverbial onion to discover cultural differences. In short, one needs to become more multicultural to manage and succeed in this world of different organizational cultures—we need to understand how "people in different cultures think, feel, and act in business, family, schools, and political organizations" (Hofstede and Hofstede, 2005).

What are the implications of this phenomenon for future research? Our recommendations are as follows:

- Research will yield more meaningful findings if conducted by teams of multicultural researchers (for example: research by Nakata and House et al., which were mentioned earlier in this book).

- Factor in or take into account culture, context, and situation: call it situational, contextual, or multicultural leadership, as we did for this book. An extended study of Lebanese executives was subsequently conducted by Muna (forthcoming 2012) to confirm or dispute the assumption that leadership is a cultural and contextual concept by looking at Lebanese-born executives working and living in three different places: Lebanon, the Gulf, and the United States. It was found that their decision-making styles and their EI leadership styles varied significantly because of the differences in context and multicultural situation in the three places. In this new edition of the book, Muna's article is reproduced in Appendix C.
- Replicate our study using a different cultural cluster; for example, with a cluster from Southeast Asia, or Latin America, or Northern Europe.
- Measure the "Ingredients for Success" for each interviewee not only by using ranking but by measuring their intensity or strength on a scale of, say, ten (for example, Self-Development is 8.7 out of 10, Ethics is 6.8, Training is 2.3, and so on).

In short, further research is needed to find out if there are any significant variations across cultures in the three stages of leadership development, the paths along the leadership journey, and in leadership styles; and how much of that variance is explained or accounted for by each of the independent variables within each culture and across cultures. We think that our research findings on developing leaders (from a Middle Eastern perspective) are indeed applicable to other societies and cultures—it is now up to future research to nullify or validate this final thought.

We end this last chapter of *Developing Multicultural Leaders* with a quotation from Winston Churchill, which could perhaps serve as a sign—or a message—along the path for aspiring leaders and for future researchers including us.

> Now this is not the end. It is not even the beginning of the end. But it is, perhaps, the end of the beginning.

Appendix A
Research Methodology and Data Analysis

Methodology

The 310 Middle Eastern leaders interviewed for this book were carefully selected to meet a number of requirements. First, the leaders came from two regions of the Middle East: six Gulf Cooperation Council (GCC) countries and six Northern Arab countries. These are countries we are most familiar with in terms of economic conditions, culture, people, and business contacts.

Second, an attempt was made to interview leaders from various types of industries (for example, nature of business, ownership, age, and size). Third, we encouraged organizations to nominate whom they consider successful leaders from all levels in their organization. The criteria for selecting successful employees were specified in the letter of invitation, which appears in Appendix B. We interviewed leaders from the upper, middle, and lower levels. Fourth, in order to obtain richer and more meaningful data, we chose a semi-structured questionnaire—thus ruling out the use of questionnaires by mail or by telephone. The Questionnaire appears in its entirety in Appendix B.

As mentioned in Chapter 8, we had our challenges with three of the 12 countries: Iraq, Palestine, and Lebanon. Iraq and Palestine were not visited because of the ongoing war in one, and the military occupation in the other. Thus, all Iraqis and Palestinians were interviewed where they live and work in the ten remaining countries. Lebanon was also a challenge because of its civil and regional wars of the past 30 years, which resulted in a recent, major "brain drain" for the country. Incidentally, this brain drain has been going on for centuries; consider the vast numbers of Lebanese living around the world—witness some of the most successful business leaders who have Lebanese parents such as Carlos Ghosn, Chairman and CEO of Renault and Nissan, or Carlos Slim Helú, the richest businessman in the world for the second year in a row, according to *Forbes*, March 2011.

Thus, for our research study, we interviewed 13 Lebanese leaders who are living and working outside their country (who were nominated by their GCC-based organizations), in addition to the 18 leaders we interviewed in Lebanon. This is reflected in the slightly larger number of Lebanese interviewed (31 leaders).

Finally, the accomplishments of all the leaders were coded into three categories: successful, excellent, and outstanding. The coding process and the relevant findings were discussed at length in Chapter 4. The answers to open-ended questions were content analyzed, and quotes from the interviewees were cited in the book at appropriate places. The interviews were conducted in confidence by a team of ten experienced Meirc consultants. The names of the leaders and their organizations will remain anonymous, as promised. The typical face-to-face interview averaged one hour and six minutes, with some lasting around two hours.

Data analysis

The data at a glance

Although much of the relevant data are found throughout the book, the following tables and charts summarize some basic data.

Individual level variables

Table A.1   **Average age by gender, level, category of leaders, and region**

Average age (N = 310) = 42 years		
Gender	Male (N = 251)	43
	Female (N = 59)	37
Level	Upper (N = 165)	46
	Middle (N = 119)	38
	Lower (N = 26)	34
Category	Outstanding (N = 89)	47
	Excellent (N = 117)	42
	Successful (N = 104)	38
Region	GCC countries (N = 174)	39
	Northern Arab countries (N = 136)	45

Table A.2 Education by location

Education	Location Arab	West	Asia	Total	%
High school or diploma	13	2	0	15	5
Bachelors	93	64	1	158	51
Post graduate (Masters or higher)	39	97	1	137	44
Total	145	163	2	310	100
Percentage	47	53	–	100	–

Organizational level variables

Table A.3 Ownership and types of business

Ownership	Number	Type	Number
Government	41	Governmental services	9
Public	8	Services & trade	53
Private	70	Oil & gas	24
International	10	Financial services	17
		Manufacturing	14
		Construction	9
		Education	3
Total	129		129

Table A.4 Size and average age of organization

Size (employees)	Number	Average age
Less than 500 employees	48	14
Between 500 and 999	14	41
1000 employees or more	67	30
Total	129	25

Table A.5 Location of education by categories of success

	Arab	West	Asia	Total
Outstanding	28	61	0	89
Excellent	51	65	1	117
Successful	66	37	1	104
Total	145	163	2	310

Table A.6   **Gender by nationality**

Nationality	Female	Male	Total
Bahraini	3	17	20
Egyptian	1	19	20
Iraqi	4	17	21
Jordanian	1	21	22
Kuwaiti	5	15	20
Lebanese	10	21	31
Omani	4	16	20
Palestinian	1	20	21
Qatari	2	19	21
Saudi Arabian	6	44	50
Syrian	5	16	21
Emirati (UAE)	17	26	43
Total	59	251	310
Percentage	19	81	100

Analysis of some variances

Table A.7   **Education level by categories of success**

	High school or high diploma	Bachelor's	Master's or higher	Total
Outstanding	2	39	48	89
Excellent	4	56	57	117
Successful	9	63	32	104
Total	15	158	137	310

Note: Chi-square = 14.5, df = 4, $p = < 0.01$.

Table A.8   **Organizational levels by categories of success**

	Upper	Middle	Lower	Total
Outstanding	72	15	2	89
Excellent	60	48	9	117
Successful	33	56	15	104
Total	165	119	26	310
Percentage %	53	38	9	100

Note: Chi-square = 47.9, df = 4, $p = < 0.01$.

Table A.9a Ten ingredients for success; (N = 310) 2010 ranking

Ranking	Mean	Ingredient for success	Standard deviation
1	(3.5)	Self-development	2.18
2	(4.4)	Ethics and values	2.77
3	(4.5)	The knowledge base	2.40
4	(4.9)	Quality of education	2.68
5	(5.1)	Early responsibility	3.06
6	(5.2)	Exposure and role models	2.68
7	(6.0)	Standards and feedback	2.58
8	(6.4)	Training opportunities	2.66
9	(6.9)	A problem-solving culture	2.53
10	(8.2)	Formal career development	1.88

Notes:

- Mean Rank (X) = total ranking score divided by total number of respondents.
- Using Friedman's test and Kendall's W test, there was significant agreement among the leaders on the ranking of the ten ingredients (Kendall's W = .208, chi-square = 581.5, df = 9, p. = 0.000).
- Other factors, very infrequently mentioned, were: surround yourself with good and qualified staff; self-knowledge; loyalty and devotion to the company; luck; "my kids"; and faith and prayer.

Table A.9b The top six ingredients for success; (N = 310) Correlation matrix

	Knowledge base	Quality of education	Self-development	Early responsibility	Exposure & role models	Ethics & values
Correlation						
Knowledge base	1.000	-0.142	-0.083	-0.322	-0.281	-0.197
Quality of education	-0.142	1.000	-0.042	0.015	-0.217	-0.110
Self-development	-0.083	-0.042	1.000	-0.009	-0.130	-0.126
Early responsibility	-0.322	0.015	-0.009	1.000	0.065	-0.098
Exposure and role models	-0.281	-0.217	-0.130	0.065	1.000	0.058
Ethics and values	-0.197	-0.110	-0.126	-0.098	0.058	1.000
Sig. (1-tailed)						
Knowledge base		0.006	0.073	0.000	0.000	0.000
Quality of education	0.006		0.233	0.394	0.000	0.026
Self-development	0.073	0.233		0.434	0.011	0.013
Early responsibility	0.000	0.394	0.434		0.127	0.043
Exposure and role models	0.000	0.000	0.011	0.127		0.152
Ethics and values	0.000	0.026	0.013	0.043	0.152	

Table A.10 Ranking of the first nine emotional intelligence (EI) competencies (Percentages)

Ranking	Accurate self-assessment	Self-confidence	Adaptability	Transparency	Achievement orientation	Initiative	Optimism	Emotional self-awareness	Emotional self-control
1	26	21	9	14	8	11	4	4	3
2	15	17	16	12	13	10	8	3	6
3	14	16	14	11	12	10	9	7	7
4	12	12	10	13	11	11	12	9	10
5	13	9	11	9	13	11	13	12	9
6	8	7	12	11	13	14	15	14	6
7	6	6	11	10	12	8	15	15	17
8	5	6	12	11	11	15	12	17	11
9	1	6	5	9	7	10	12	19	31
Total	100	100	100	100	100	100	100	100	100

Table A.11 Ranking of the second nine EI competencies (Percentages)

Ranking	Inspirational leadership	Team work and collaboration	Developing others	Organizational awareness	Change catalyst	Influence	Service orientation	Empathy	Conflict management
1	33	22	6	11	5	4	9	9	1
2	17	16	16	10	10	13	9	6	3
3	12	15	19	7	13	9	8	8	9
4	7	15	15	10	14	15	9	7	8
5	8	12	14	12	11	12	11	13	7
6	9	7	13	14	10	10	13	12	12
7	6	7	8	11	13	11	13	14	17
8	4	4	8	13	12	14	15	14	16
9	4	2	1	12	12	12	13	17	27
Total	100	100	100	100	100	100	100	100	100%

Appendix B
The Semi-Structured Questionnaire and Invitation Letter to Organizations

The Semi-Structured Questionnaire

Date: _____   Start: _____

Code: _____   Finish: _____

Interviewer: _____   Duration: _____

Meirc Research Study

(Confidential, no name)

Country: _____
(Please circle one)

Ownership: Government   Public   Private   International

Industry: Government   Services & Trade   Oil & Gas

Financial Services   Manufacturing   Construction

Name of Organization: _____

Size of Organization: <500   500–999   >1,000 employees

Date of establishment (approximate): _____

Nationality: Bahraini   Kuwaiti   Omani
Qatari   Saudi Arabian   UAE

Egyptian   Iraqi   Jordanian   Lebanese
Palestinian   Syrian

Age: _____   **Male** ☐   **Female** ☐

Education: High School/Diploma   Bachelor's
Master's or Higher

187

Major/Field: _____

Country of Education: _____

Department: _____

Current Position: _____   Top ☐   Mid ☐   Low ☐

PART I

(Interview note: Use opposite page for additional space)

1. What are your principal accomplishments/contributions in the past 3 to 4 years? (Check out: Developing Nationals, Cost/Productivity Improvements, Organizational Objectives/Goals, etc).

2. What talents, skills and abilities helped you in achieving the above?

3. How did you develop these? (When, how and where did you develop them? Were you born with them?)

4. What were the factors, people, or events that contributed to your career? (Check out: Education, Courses, Bosses, Job, Luck, and Crises)

The following were found to contribute to the acquisition of superior skills, knowledge and attitudes. Kindly, rank in order of their importance to **your** success in life/management.

Please rank from 1 (most important) to 11 (least important).
(Do not skip or repeat any ranking)

Ranking

_____   A.   Training (courses and on-the-job training)

_____   B.   Current or previous manager(s): their positive support and encouragement

_____ C. Practical on the job experience, and technical knowledge

_____ D. Quality of education received (including extra curricular activities)

_____ E. Self-development: a thirst for continuous learning

_____ F. Organizational climate and culture, which encourages learning

_____ G. Early responsibility (at home and work)

_____ H. Exposure and role models: Learning from persons whom you respect and admire. Learning from others through exposure and travel.

_____ I. Formal career development programs provided by the organization.

_____ J. Work ethics and values: hard work, integrity, commitment to work, and quality of work.

_____ K. Other (Please describe): _____

_____

PART II

1. The effective manager is the one who: (circle one answer only)

I. Usually makes his or her own decisions, but later explains his reasons for making these decisions.

II. Usually consults with his or her subordinates before making decisions; their opinion may or may not influence his decisions.

III. Usually meets with subordinates when there is an important decision to be made. Puts the problem before them and invites discussion. Accepts the majority viewpoint as the decision.

IV. Usually asks his or her subordinates to make decisions, and holds them fully accountable for the outcome of these decisions.

2. Now, for the above types of managers, please mark the one which you would **prefer** to work under (circle one answer only):

I II III IV

3. And, to which one of the four types of managers would you say your own **manager** most closely corresponds? (circle one answer only):

I II III IV

PART III

Working with Multinationals and Expatriates

A. **What are the most challenging aspects of working with multinational organizations? (If applicable).**

_____

_____

_____

_____

_____

B.	CHARACTERISTICS YOU LIKE MOST	CHARACTERISTICS YOU DISLIKE MOST
Western Expats	1. _____ 2. _____ 3. _____	1. _____ 2. _____ 3. _____
Arab Expats	1. _____ 2. _____ 3. _____	1. _____ 2. _____ 3. _____

Asian	1. _____	1. _____
Expats	2. _____	2. _____
	3. _____	3. _____

PART IV

A. The following 9 statements describe how successful leaders manage themselves.

Kindly rank them in order of their importance to your success in life and/or career.

Please rank them from 1 (most important) to 9 (least important). (Do not skip or repeat any ranking)

Ranking		Statement
_____	A.	I recognize how my feelings affect my performance and the performance of others.

أدرك مدى تأثير عواطفي على مستوى أدائي وأداء الآخرين.

| _____ | B. | I see opportunities and take action to make the most of these opportunities. |

أنتهز الفرص وأبادر في استغلالها بشكل جيد.

| _____ | C. | I understand my own strengths and limitations and welcome constructive feedback to improve. |

أدرك نقاط القوة والضعف الخاصة بي وأرحب بالتغذية العكسية.

| _____ | D. | I am ready to act and seize possibilities for a better future. |

أسعى لاستغلال الفرص من أجل مستقبل أفضل.

| _____ | E. | I am confident and self-assured, and I know my abilities. |

لدي ثقة بالنفس وأتمتع بالمقدرة على فهم قدراتي.

| _____ | F. | I control bad moods and emotional impulses. |

أتحكم بالعواطف الثائرة والمزاجات السيئة.

_____ G. I have personal standards that drive me to seek performance improvement.

لدي معايير شخصية تدفعني لتحسين الأداء.

_____ H. I behave in accordance with my values.

أتصرف تبعا لقيمي الذاتية.

_____ I. I am flexible in adapting to changing situations.

لدي مرونة في التأقلم مع المواقف المتغيرة.

B. Here are the top 2 rankings you have selected. Can you please give me specific examples on how one or both of these rankings play out in your personal and/or professional life?

Ranking 1:
Example   _____
_____
_____
_____
_____
_____
_____

Ranking 2:
Example   _____
_____
_____
_____
_____
_____

A. Now, the next 9 competencies describe how successful leaders manage relationships.

Rank them in order of their importance to your success in life and/or career. Please rank them from 1 (most important) to 9 (least important).

(Do not skip or repeat any ranking)

Ranking	Competency	Explanation
_____	A. Empathy التعاطف	: Understanding and showing sensitivity to people's feelings. فهم أحاسيس الآخرين وإدراك مشاعرهم.
_____	B. Organizational Awareness الوعي التنظيمي (المؤسساتي)	: Appreciating the values, culture, and social networks within the organization. احترام القيم والثقافات والشبكات الاجتماعية على اختلافها داخل المؤسسة.
_____	C. Service Orientation الاهتمام بالخدمة	: Recognizing and meeting the needs of the follower, client or customer. تلبية حاجات العملاء الداخليين والخارجيين.
_____	D. Inspirational Leadership القيادة الملهمة	: Moving people toward a common vision or a shared mission. حث الاشخاص نحو تحقيق رؤية مشتركة وهدف واحد.
_____	E. Developing Others تطوير مهارات الآخرين	: Cultivating people's abilities by guiding them and offering feedback. تطوير قدرات الغير وتقديم النصيحة لهم والتغذية العكسية
_____	F. Influence التأثير على الآخرين	: Using a wide variety of tactics for persuading and engaging a group. استعمال أساليب ووسائل مختلفة للاقناع والتأثير على الغير.
_____	G. Change Catalyst التحفيز على التغيير	: Initiating and managing change. المبادرة بعملية التغيير وإدارتها.
_____	H. Conflict Management إدارة الخلافات	: Bringing conflict out in the open and managing it. إظهار الخلافات وإدارتها بشفافية.
_____	I. Team Work & Collaboration العمل الجماعي والتعاون	: Drawing others into active and enthusiastic commitment to the collective effort. اشراك الآخرين وتحفيزهم للالتزام بالعمل الجماعي.

Here are the top 2 competencies you have selected.

_____,   _____.

Please cite specific examples on how one or both of these competencies play out in your personal/professional life.

Competency 1:
Example _____

_____

_____

Competency 2:
Example _____

_____

_____

A.   Leadership Styles

Below are 6 leadership styles followed by an explanation of the style and the "style in a phrase" describing it.

Style 1		Leader moves people toward shared dreams. **"Come with me."**
Style 2		Leader connects what a person wants with the organization's goals. **"Try this."**
Style 3		Leader gives clear directions to calm fears whenever necessary. **"Do what I tell you."**
Style 4		Leader values people's input and gets their commitment through participation. **"What do you think?"**
Style 5		Leader meets challenging and exciting goals. **"Do as I do now."**
Style 6		Leader connects people to each other. **"People come first."**

Two questions:

1.   **Select from the above <u>your primary</u> style (most often used) and a backup style (occasionally used)?**
     Primary _____   **Backup** _____

2. From the above 6 styles, which two are the most typical/frequent style(s) used by <u>your manager</u>?

_____   _____

Please cite an example of how and when you have used your primary (most often used) style?

_____
_____
_____

Please cite an example of an instance when you may have used your backup style?

_____
_____
_____

What <u>advice</u> would you give younger future leaders/managers so they can be more effective or successful?

_____
_____
_____
_____

A final question:

Why do you think that <u>some</u> leaders are more successful than others?

_____
_____
_____
_____
_____
_____

Thank you

Invitation Letter

This letter was sent to carefully selected organizations inviting them to nominate their most successful leaders. We are aware that some of the leaders that were nominated could not participate in this study due to problems in logistics, timing, or availability.

Dear ....,

Meirc Training & Consulting has launched a major research study starting May 2009. The aim of this research project is to investigate the current state of leadership and management development in the Gulf and Northern Arab regions through a study of successful managers and leaders in these regions. Of course, the ultimate benefit of this research is to contribute to the advancement of knowledge in this field.

Over the last 50 years, **Meirc Training & Consulting** has conducted management research in the Gulf during the 1960s, 1970s, 1980s and 1990s. Our vision is to continue this tradition, which we believe will eventually be of great benefit to our clients and to the future organizational leaders.

The plan is to interview a large number of successful managers and supervisors from various industries and sectors in the six GCC countries, as well as from six Northern Arab countries (Egypt, Iraq, Jordan, Lebanon, Palestine, and Syria). These interviews will be conducted face-to-face by our experienced consultants, and each interview will take just over one hour to complete. **To ensure complete confidentiality and anonymity, there will be no attempt to identify in the published results the respondents by name.** Only the Meirc researchers will have access to the completed interview questionnaire.

The Meirc research project will be directed by our Chairman, Dr. Farid A. Muna, and by our partner, Dr. Ziad A. Zennie, both of whom have extensive experience in management research.

Your organization has been selected as one of the organizations to be included in the research, and we would greatly appreciate the nomination of up to 6 (six) of your employees who meet the selection criteria, shown on the following page.

The research project has a number of benefits. To list only a few, it will provide direction and have recommendations for:

- the advancement of our knowledge on the crucial topic of leadership.
- recruitment practices of potential "successful" leaders
- the design and implementation of effective succession planning systems
- talent management and leadership development of high potentials targeted for promotion and / or transfer.

Your cooperation will be highly appreciated.

Yours sincerely,

Dr. Ramsey Hakim
Managing Director

Criteria for Self Nomination and/or Selecting Employees for the Meirc Research

Please use the following criteria as guidelines for nominating your executives, managers, or supervisors (**only nationals of the GCC & the following Arab countries: Egypt, Iraq, Jordan, Lebanon, Palestine, and Syria**):

1. Is considered an effective leader and a role model for future managers.
2. Has high concern for mentoring or developing younger nationals.
3. Has a good reputation and track record (integrity, honesty, and hard work) both in the organization and the community.
4. Has made significant accomplishments and contributions in the past three to four years through:

- Passion for the job; and/or
- Productivity/cost improvements in his or her area of responsibility; and/or
- Enhancement of organizational goals, objectives, or vision.

Kindly, reply with the required information in the table below.

Name of Participating Organizations:	

	Name	Position	Email	Telephone Number
1				
2				
3				
4				
5				
6				

For further queries:
Dr. Ziad A. Zennie,
Meirc Training & Consulting
Tel: 00971 4 334 5858, Fax: 00971 4 334 5440
P.O. Box 5883, Dubai, UAE
Email: zzennie@meirc.com

Appendix C
The Extended Study of
Lebanese Executives

The following article by Farid Muna will be published in the *Journal of Management Development*, 2012, Vol. 31, No. 1. It is reproduced here after some editing in order to minimize duplication with the text of this book.

"Contextual Leadership: A Study of Lebanese Executives Working in Lebanon, the GCC Countries, and the United States"

What happens, one wonders, if executives who were born and raised in one country decide to live and work in a different country and in an environment where their followers are more diverse, multicultural, or multinational? Will these executives adapt their leadership styles and practices to fit the new situation in order to be successful? Or will they impose their own culture and style on the new organizational environment? These are the questions that prompted this study, and the research findings will endeavor to answer.

In brief, would the indigenous cultural attitudes and leadership behavior of executives change if and when contexts and situations change? It is encouraging to read what Jackson and Parry (2008) wrote, "In effect, by bringing context into the analysis we are suggesting that the 'when' and 'where' questions should be given a lot more prominence when we study leadership."

Muna and Zennie (2010) in their book, *Developing Multicultural Leaders*, corroborate the significance of culture and context after conducting a field research by interviewing 310 successful Middle Eastern leaders from 12 countries from 129 organizations. They found that culture, context, and situation have a significant impact on the emotional intelligence (EI) competencies, the EI leadership styles, and the decision-making styles of the leaders they interviewed.

This article builds upon and expands that field research. However, it focuses on only one of the 12 nationalities, the Lebanese. It enlarges the original sample of Lebanese executives working in Lebanon and the six Gulf Cooperation Council (GCC) countries, and it adds a third group of Lebanese executives who are living and working in the United States.

Culture, context, and situation do matter

Cross-cultural leadership research has become, in the past few decades, a subject of great interest given that the world is "shrinking" and becoming more "globalized." One of the earliest monumental studies was conducted in 49 countries by Geert Hofstede (1980). His findings were influential and interesting; his conclusion: culture and societal values do matter when it comes to leadership styles and management practices. Hofstede measured five dimensions (originally, only the first four were used) to study culture: individualism–collectivism; power distance; uncertainty avoidance; masculinity–femininity; and time orientation. He described culture as the "collective programming of the mind," and "software of the mind" (Hofstede, 2001).

Hofstede's work was expanded and replicated by an equally monumental work covering 62 societies by House *et al.* (2004), known as the GLOBE project. Both studies have been criticized recently, namely for their Western-based conceptualization of leadership, and for certain aspects of their methodology and research approach. Interestingly, the criticism is not restricted to other outside scholars, but comes from Hofstede and the GLOBE researchers themselves. The GLOBE scholars wrote in the abstract of a 2006 article:

> We show why there is no theoretical or empirical basis for Hofstede's criticism that GLOBE measures of values are too abstract or for his contention that national and organizational cultures are phenomena of different order. We also show why Hofstede has a limited understanding of the relationship between national wealth and culture. Furthermore, we explain why Hofstede's reanalysis of the GLOBE data is inappropriate and produces incomprehensible results.
>
> Javidan *et al.*, 2006

On the other hand, other criticism of Hofstede's and GLOBE's approaches were voiced by Dickson *et al.* (2003), Dickson *et al.*

(2009), and Nakata (2009) who have called for a different, more dynamic, interdisciplinary, and contextual approach for studying cross-cultural leadership. In *Beyond Hofstede*, Nakata urges researchers to start on a new journey, using different paradigms:

> While the trend is promising in that researchers are honing in on culture as a way of comprehending global economic and market transformations, it also points to a maturing line of inquiry that would benefit from an expansion of culture paradigms. The near-exclusive adoption of the Hofstedean view means that business researchers have agreed that it captures as a phenomenon all that culture is. Convergence on a single paradigm should signal arriving at the end of a journey of discovery. However, because few alternative views have been investigated, the journey has in fact just begun.
>
> Nakata, 2009

There are some scholars who are advocating convergence in the multiple and often-conflicting models of cross-cultural research. Nardon and Steers (2009), for example, state, "However, a problem that continues to plague organizational researchers in this area is a lack of convergence across these models. This divergence represents what we refer to as the *culture theory jungle* – a situation in which researchers must choose between competing, if sometimes overlapping, models to further their research goals and then defend such choices against a growing body of critics."

The problem, as seen by this author, is not one of divergence or convergence across completely different paradigms or models, but rather it is an internal competition within the *same* "jungle" in which these models are based on more or less the same Western-based conceptualization of cross-cultural leadership. It is believed that leadership is contextual, place-based, and situational; and that *effective* leaders do in fact adapt their styles and practices to new cultures no matter which original culture they come from.

Thus, it would be more fruitful if researchers shift their focus and efforts to the more beneficial quest of how best to develop multicultural leaders who can effectively work within and across national borders, as well as effectively lead followers who come from diverse or different cultures. The so-called cultural barriers are opportunities and challenges to explore and understand rather than be perceived as problematic obstacles just because cultures are different and do not neatly fit certain models of leadership.

Consider, for instance, five multicultural executives who were born, raised, and educated in different parts of the world and who are leading large multinational companies: Dr. Ray Irani (Lebanese) of Occidental Petroleum; Sir Howard Stringer (Welsh) of Sony Corporation; Indra Nooyi (Indian) of PepsiCo; Fred Hassan (Pakistani) of Bausch and Lomb; and Carlos Ghosn (French, Brazilian-born son of Lebanese parents) of Renault Nissan.

Some Anglo-Dutch companies (for example, Shell Oil, Unilever, and Reckitt Benckiser) are also managed by multicultural executives who consider their companies as multi-country and global. In a recent *Harvard Business Review* article, the CEO of Reckitt Benckiser, which operates in over 60 countries, wrote:

> Now in every country we have people of many nationalities as well as local citizens. Today an Italian is running the UK business, and an American is running the German business. A Dutchman is running the U.S. business, an Indian the Chinese business, a Belgian the Brazilian business, and a Frenchman the Russian business. It is not that you can't advance at RB in your local company. You can. But we also offer unique global mobility and experience to people who want to grow their careers on a world stage.
>
> Becht, *HBR*, April 2010

Jackson and Parry rightly make a solid case for taking into account culture, context, and situation when studying leadership. Jackson, a professor of leadership at the University of Auckland Business School, coined the "Geography of Leadership" concept, a most appropriate and highly descriptive name. He and his co-author advocate that, "The place where and the time in which leadership is created influences how the leaders and followers go about co-producing leadership" (Jackson and Parry, 2008). They comment on the GLOBE research with these words:

> The GLOBE project represents a bold and ambitious step towards broadening the empirical net of leadership research but its theoretical base is still firmly rooted in American soil. We gain a great deal in methodological rigour but lose something in

philosophical acuity. House's intentions are unquestionably honourable when he asserts, 'Hopefully, GLOBE will be able to liberate organizational behaviour from the US hegemony' (2004: xxv). However, we feel that, somewhat perversely, American supremacy in this field is strengthened by this project not challenged.

A comparative study of Lebanese executives

For this study, a total of 76 Lebanese successful executives were interviewed: 27 living and working in Lebanon, 24 in the six Gulf countries, and 25 in the United States. These executives were nominated by their organizations in Lebanon and the Gulf because of their achievements and success as leaders. The US sample was carefully chosen by the author based on their accomplishments as successful executives and their good reputation in the community. The executives from the US were chosen from the East Coast, Midwest, South, and West Coast; they were interviewed either in person, by telephone, through Skype, or by email. All others in Lebanon and the Gulf were interviewed in person.

The three groups of successful executives represented in this study came from several types of organizations: finance and banking, manufacturing, construction, educational foundations, services and trade. Their organizations were chosen carefully to include private, public, regional, and international organizations.

This study endeavors to confirm or dispute the assumption that leadership is a cultural and contextual concept by looking at Lebanese-born executives working and living in three different places. Our premise is that Lebanese executives will adjust and adapt their leadership style in order to be successful with their new, more diverse, and more multicultural followers—in their new environments. The study examines (a) early ingredients for success, (b) decision-making styles, and (c) EI leadership styles.

Early ingredients for success

The Lebanese executives were asked to rank in order of importance ten ingredients for success, which earlier studies had established as necessary ingredients for leadership success (Meirc, 1989; Muna, 2003; and Muna and Zennie, 2010). The first five of these ingredients are related to early life experiences; the second five to experiences after one starts a career (for all ten ingredients, see Table C.1). The first five early ingredients for success are:

- **Self development** is the insatiable thirst and passion for continuous learning throughout life—and the acknowledgement and desire for self-improvement as vital for success.
- **Ethics and values** refer to the work ethics of hard and honest work, and that quality and excellence in one's work do matter.
- **Quality of education** describes the richness of the experience gained while receiving knowledge; the stretching of the mind; and participation in extra-curricular activities that teach social and leadership skills.
- **Early responsibility** refers to being responsible and accountable, starting from early childhood, either out of necessity or as a deliberate part of child upbringing.
- **Exposure and role models** relate to the idea of learning from other people and cultures; and learning from people one considers as role models.

Together with these five ingredients, research strongly suggests that early life events and crises (be they happy or traumatic) have considerable impact on the making of successful leaders (Bennis, 2009). In fact Bennis calls these experiences "crucibles" and "transformative experiences," and it is through these early experiences that leaders discover their authentic selves and thus become effective.

As expected, the five early ingredients for success, which are usually learned during childhood and educational years, were fairly similar for all three groups of executives; after all, they were born and raised in the same place and culture, Lebanon (see Table C.1). The exception was "exposure and role models," which ranked significantly higher for executives working and living outside Lebanon. These executives were exposed to different cultures and are currently working with more diverse followers. Additionally, many of them mentioned the positive influence of their bosses—their role models—when they started working overseas.

The order of the rankings of the ten ingredients is also not surprising since much of the recent literature points to the significant impact that early life experiences have on leadership potential (for example, Bennis, 2009; Muna and Zennie, 2010). The second five

Table C.1 Ingredients for success for three Lebanese groups (N=76) rankings (1=most important, 10=least important)

Ingredient for success	Lebanon		Gulf		USA	
	Mean	Rank	Mean	Rank	Mean	Rank
Self development	2.7	1	2.9	1	3.3	2
Ethics and values	3.7	2	3.8	2	2.9	1
Early responsibility	4.4	3	5.0	4	4.6	4
The knowledge base	4.7	4	5.1	5	5.8	6
Quality of education	5.5	5	5.2	6	5.0	5
Standards and feedback (from boss)	5.6	6	6.3	7	6.2	7
Exposure and role models	5.8	7	4.0	3	4.5	3
Training opportunities	7.0	8	6.5	8	7.2	9
A problem-solving culture	7.5	9	7.6	9	6.9	8
Formal career development	8.4	10	8.7	10	8.8	10

ingredients become available later on in life shortly after a potential leader starts a career; they are provided by the immediate manager and the organization.

Decision-making styles

For the current study, we utilized a power-sharing continuum that was used by many management researchers in the past (Vroom 2000; Muna, 1980; Meirc, 1989; Muna, 2003; Muna and Zennie, 2010). Decision-making style was defined and measured on a four-point equal interval scale reflecting various degrees of power sharing. The four decision-making styles on the continuum were discussed earlier in Chapter 8, on page 123.

Own decision Style I	Consultation Style II	Joint decision Style III	Delegation Style IV

The leaders we interviewed were asked to indicate which of the four styles:

(a) They felt is usually the *most effective*,
(b) They *preferred to work under*, and
(c) They felt their *own manager's style* most closely corresponded to.

Table C.2 "Most effective" decision-making styles by region (N = 76) (expressed in percentages)

Region	Style I	Style II	Style III	Style IV	Total
Lebanon (N = 27)	0	81	19	0	100
Gulf (N = 24)	0	54	42	4	100
USA (N = 25)	0	40	48	12	100

Chi-square = 11.1, df = 6, p. = 0.085.

Table C.3 "Prefer to work under" decision-making styles by region (N = 76) (expressed in percentages)

Region	Style I	Style II	Style III	Style IV	Total
Lebanon (N = 27)	0	81	15	4	100
Gulf (N = 24)	0	46	33	21	100
USA (N = 25)	0	40	44	16	100

Chi-square = 11.5, df = 6, p. = 0.074.

Table C.4 "Own manager's" decision-making styles by region (N = 76) (expressed in percentages)

Region	Style I	Style II	Style III	Style IV	Total
Lebanon (N = 27)	32	48	12	8	100
Gulf (N = 24)	8	42	25	25	100
USA (N = 25)	5	33	33	29	100

Chi-square = 12.5, df = 6, p. = 0.053.

Tables C.2, C.3, and C.4 summarize the data for Lebanese leaders in the three regions and their responses on the three decision-making styles: most effective, prefer to work under, and own manager's styles.

Clearly, there are statistically significant differences among the three groups: Lebanese leaders living and working outside Lebanon are more participative in their decision-making styles; and their own managers are also less autocratic.

Consultation (Style II) in the Middle East is an expected and acceptable decision-making style (Muna, 1980; Muna and Zennie, 2010; Ali, 2005). In both Styles I and II, the decisions are made by the leader. Thus, if we combine Styles I and II shown in Table C.2 (most effective styles), where the final decisions are made by one person, the results become far more insightful and interesting.

Table C.5 Autocratic vs. participative styles Lebanese leaders, in Lebanon (N = 27) (expressed in percentages)

	Autocratic-consultative (Styles I & II)	Participative (Styles III & IV)
Most effective	81	19
Prefer (to work under)	81	19
Own manager's	80	20

Table C.6 Autocratic vs. participative styles Lebanese leaders, in GCC countries (N = 24) (expressed in percentages)

	Autocratic-consultative (Styles I & II)	Participative (Styles III & IV)
Most effective	54	46
Prefer (to work under)	46	54
Own manager's	50	50

Table C.7 Autocratic vs. participative styles Lebanese leaders, in USA (N = 25) (expressed in percentages)

	Autocratic-consultative (Styles I & II)	Participative (Styles III & IV)
Most effective	40	60
Prefer (to work under)	40	60
Own manager's	38	62

The autocratic-consultative styles (I and II) are compared with the participative styles (III and IV) and are shown in Tables C.5, C.6, and C.7, for the three groups of Lebanese leaders.

Once again, the data show that leaders who are living and working in the Gulf and the United States are by far more participative than their successful counterparts in Lebanon. It is believed that much of this variance is due to the differences in context, situation, and place.

EI leadership styles

Research on competencies suggests that success in life and at work depends not only on intelligence quotient (IQ) but requires certain emotional intelligence (EI) competencies. Building on earlier research, Goleman (1995) and Goleman *et al.* (2002) have identified 18 EI competencies. Furthermore, Goleman argued that these competencies, if used effectively, will impact the EI leadership styles of managers. Six leadership styles were identified by Goleman *et al.*, each springing from different components of emotional intelligence, and each style builds resonance (positive impact) or dissonance (negative impact) with followers and hence impacts the climate of an organization. The six leadership styles are:

- **Visionary**: moves people towards shared dreams (Resonant style: highly positive impact on climate)
- **Coaching**: connects individual wants with the organization's goals (Resonant: positive impact)
- **Affiliative**: creates harmony by connecting people to each other (Resonant: positive impact)
- **Democratic**: values people's inputs and gets commitment through participation (Resonant: positive impact)
- **Pacesetting**: meets challenging and exciting goals (Dissonant: negative impact, but useful under certain conditions when there is a need to get quick results)
- **Commanding**: soothes fears by giving clear direction in an emergency (Dissonant: negative impact, but useful under certain conditions such as in a crisis, or to kick-start a turnaround, or with problem employees).

Goleman further argues that effective leaders should use all six styles depending on the situation and context (the last two—pacesetting and commanding—have a negative impact on climate, but may be applied with caution and under specific conditions or situations). Goleman's research showed that leaders who are able to master four or more styles, and have the ability to change styles as situations change, often generate superior performance from their people.

Goleman's research was replicated in other cultures. A few of the more recent studies have found that the EI competencies and EI leadership styles in other cultures and contexts do not necessarily correspond to the US-based findings. For instance, Muna and Zennie (2010) investigated Middle Eastern executives; Ilangovan and colleagues (2007) found considerable differences between styles of Indian and American managers; and Leung (2005) found that Western EI model of open and participative leadership clashed with the cultural values of Chinese managers. Leaders and followers in other cultures interact differently: their values and expectations differ, and leaders use different styles that are more congruent with their own cultural values.

In fact, Dickson *et al.* (2003) speculated several years ago that it may be "the beginnings of the decline" in the search for universal leadership principles that apply unvaryingly across all cultures. They wrote:

> . . . the recognition that much leadership theory has a distinctly American bias has made some researchers particularly interested in unique ways in which leadership manifests itself in other cultures. An example of non-Western style of leadership that is valued and found in many developing nations is paternalism . . . However, culture specific non-Western models are not always presented in international journals. In addition, much research assesses whether a model developed elsewhere is also applicable in a different context or compares the effects of a set of behaviors in different cultures rather than starting to build new models from the unique vantage points of a specific culture.

Research findings support the views of Dickson and his colleagues. For example, leadership in the Middle East can be *generally* described by three characteristics; stated in a summary form, for the sake of space.

- **Paternalism**: one can substitute this phrase using others such as: tribal, familial, or clannish leadership styles. The manager is often regarded as a "father", an "uncle", or "older brother". This paternalistic style is not restricted to family businesses, but can be observed in most other organizations (Muna, 1980; Muna, 2003; Ali, 2005; Yahchouchi, 2009).
- **Personalized Approach**: preference for personal over impersonal approach; emotions and feelings do matter; personal factors are taken in considerations, including the use of connections or *wastah*; trust and loyalty are often as important as efficiency.
- **Autocratic-Consultative Decision Making**: decisions are made by higher level managers and executives, after frequent consultation;

Table C.8   **Primary and backup leadership styles and region (percentage choosing top two styles) (respondent's style)**

Region	Visionary	Coaching	Affiliative	Democratic	Pace-setting	Com-manding	Total
Lebanon	30%	7%	13%	26%	9%	15%	100%
GCC	21%	23%	11%	29%	8%	8%	100%
USA	20%	30%	4%	40%	2%	4%	100%

Table C.9   **Manager's primary and backup leadership styles and region (percentage choosing top two styles) (own manager's style)**

Region	Visionary	Coaching	Affiliative	Democratic	Pace-setting	Com-manding	Total
Lebanon	18%	19%	10%	21%	14%	18%	100%
GCC	24%	14%	7%	19%	17%	19%	100%
USA	17%	20%	7%	38%	5%	13%	100%

delegation is not often used (Meirc, 1989; Muna, 2003; Muna and Zennie, 2010).

The 76 Lebanese leaders were first asked to select *their* primary (most often used) EI and their backup leadership styles. The results are shown in Tables C.8. A chi-square test shows significant differences among the leadership styles of the Lebanese in the three regions (chi-square = 18.1, df = 10, p. = 0.051).

Pacesetting and commanding styles are both dissonant styles and have a negative impact on employees and performance, but are useful under certain conditions as mentioned above. If we add these two styles the results become more interesting: 24 per cent in Lebanon, 16 per cent in the GCC countries, and 6 per cent in the USA. Although respondents were not asked the nationality of followers, it is likely that they were non-Lebanese in both the GCC countries and in the Unites States. On the other hand, if we add the highest ranking styles (visionary and democratic, both with positive impact), the results are: 56 per cent in Lebanon, 50 per cent in the GCC countries, and 60 per cent in the USA.

Respondents were then asked to describe the primary and backup styles of their *managers*, if they had any (a few entrepreneurs did not report to a direct manager). The results are shown in Table C.9.

There were no significant differences in the managers' leadership styles (chi-square = 9.37, df =10, p. = 0.498).

There was, however, a noticeable decrease in the combined total of pacesetting and commanding styles: 32 per cent in Lebanon, 36 per cent in the GCC countries, and 18 per cent in the USA. This decrease in these two autocratic styles was accompanied by an increase in the visionary and democratic styles: 39 per cent in Lebanon, 43 per cent in the GCC countries, and 55 per cent in the USA.

Mastering the cultural context

In addition to the quantitative data collected during the interviews (discussed above), the successful Lebanese executives were asked a number of open-ended questions. Examples of the open-ended questions include: "What talents, skills, and abilities helped you achieve success in your life and career(s) so far?" "How did you develop these?" "What were the factors, people, or events that contributed to your career?" "Why do you think that some leaders are more successful than others?" The answers provided valuable insights into the reasons for the success of executives who stayed in Lebanon and those who went "overseas."

Three recurring themes were heard from these successful executives:

- Ability to adapt to new situations and cultures, and to work well with different nationalities; and the ability to learn from adversity (being forced to leave their war-torn country);
- The great impact of role models (most mentioned were parents, or bosses and mentors at work upon arrival to a new country); and
- Integrity, dedication, early responsibility, and hard work directed towards high ambitions and goals.

Perhaps a few representative quotations from the interviews of successful executives working and living in the three regions will illustrate the themes.

USA: "I would estimate that around 25 per cent of all the Lebanese who came over to the United States are extremely successful. First, they adjusted well; and they have had integrity, high ambitions and goals; and second, they worked extremely hard. The other

75 per cent never really adjusted. They stuck to the old mentality, attributing their setbacks to prejudice, to bad luck, or to the environment and to circumstances."

USA: "My parents taught me integrity and honesty, my friends taught me how to communicate and debate and to stay focused on what matters. The civil war in Lebanon taught me volunteering, survival, and courage. These skills are the foundations that helped me succeed after I left Lebanon."

USA: "In USA, business is business—much less personal or emotional than back home!"

USA: "Loyalty, honesty, hard work, respect for others, and the drive to excel—these factors enabled me to succeed. Also, I was lucky to have a strong and phenomenal mentor (my role model) who helped me in my early years. In short, the crisis in Lebanon led to the opportunity to be in the USA, and, thus being in the right place at the right time."

GCC: "Flexibility: I adapt quickly to different situations, and can deal with all kinds of people and nationalities; a must when working in the UAE."

GCC: "I built my skills through interacting with different cultures, mainly in Lebanon and the USA, and then I came to Saudi Arabia where one works with people from many different cultures. In brief, my multicultural background helped me a lot."

Lebanon: "Two main events influenced my life and career: First, going through the civil war, seeing displaced people suffer, helping them build tents and shelters . . . seeing and feeling the pain of others. Second, going to Harvard University where we learned more from colleagues (from 70 countries) than from our professors. Both experiences were valuable when I returned to work in Lebanon."

Lebanon: "I was fortunate to have studied in the USA, and to have started my career with the largest Western bank. By the age of 30, I came back to Lebanon and put all that experience to work."

This study confirms that the executives we interviewed succeeded in life and in business for three main reasons: First, the early ingredients of self development and of strong work ethics, which were ranked first and second highest by *all* three groups. Second, for those who left Lebanon, their exposure to different cultures and people, and their role models played a significant part in their success. Third, again for those who left Lebanon, they were aided by their ability to adapt to, and master the new context, and to overcome the adversity of leaving a war-torn or and turbulent homeland.

In *Crucibles of Leadership*, Thomas (2008) describes the experiences of leaders he interviewed as ". . . transformative events that occurred outside their professional lives as often as they cited ones that happened on the job. The most profound among those experiences—the *crucibles* that led to a new or an altered sense of identity—were nested in family life, wartime trauma, athletic competition, and/or personal loss far more often than in work assignments."

McCall and Hollenbeck (2002) concluded that gaining international experience is the determining factor for success, and that the most important prerequisites are the capacity and willingness to learn from that experience. The successful Lebanese executives seem to have done just that—they had the capacity and willingness to learn from the experience of working outside their country. Their adaptability, cultural sensitivity, and resilience contributed to their success.

Summary

This study compared three groups of successful Lebanese-born executives working in three parts of the world: Lebanon, GCC countries, and the United States. They shared the early ingredients of success, with the exception of those outside Lebanon who ranked exposure and role models much higher in terms of importance.

Their decision-making styles differed significantly. Those working in multicultural, diverse countries were significantly more participative and thus much less autocratic than those executives working with Lebanese followers. Finally, the EI leadership styles of those working outside Lebanon were significantly different.

There were no statistically significant differences between decision-making and leadership styles and the other variables such as age, gender, or the type, size, and ownership of the organizations in which these Lebanese executives worked.

This study lends further support to the notion that successful leaders adapt to their new culture and context; they learn from experience and adversity; and they are able to master the context in order to achieve their goals through hard work, determination, and perseverance.

Implications for future research

Warren Bennis cites adaptive capacity or resilience in leaders who master contexts as one of the keys to great leadership. He, it seems, was referring to organizational contexts, or leadership in a national context, or time contexts; this article, on the other hand, emphasizes cultural contexts and the adaptive capacity of Lebanese leaders to adjust to the cultural contexts of their new organizational environments and their diverse followers.

The research findings of this study strongly suggest that future cross-cultural research would be more fruitful if directed towards more practical quests, namely:

- Helping multinational organizations develop future multicultural leaders to effectively lead followers who are becoming increasingly more diverse and multinational; and where context and situation do matter.
- Redefining global organizational strategies whose objectives are "crossing borders in a world where differences still matter." (Ghemawat, 2007); and concentrating on developing an array of strategies that go well beyond the one-size-fits-all mindset.
- Taking into account culture, context and place, and situation when studying leadership styles and practices within a certain culture and across cultures. Such studies would ideally be conducted by a team of multicultural and interdisciplinary researchers.
- Specifically, future research should be conducted with groups of other nationalities; for example, with executives born and raised in Europe, or India, or China, or South America, and so on, who are living and working in different parts of the world. Such future research will confirm or dispute the findings of this study, namely, that leadership is contextual.

Over 40 years ago, Karlene Roberts (1970) came to this conclusion after reviewing cross-cultural research: "Organizations are rarely viewed as parts of their environments; yet understanding organizational-environmental interactions seems a major practical reason for engaging in cross-cultural research." Roberts went on to urge scholars that: ". . . more effort be invested in understanding behavior in a single culture, developing middle-level theories to guide explorations, and seeking the relevant questions to ask across cultures."

We need this type of three-dimensional perspective to fully understand and appreciate the dynamics of leadership across cultures. It is only appropriate to end with these wise words from two cultural anthropologists, written many years ago:

> *Every person is in certain respects:*
> *a. Like all other persons*
> *b. Like some other persons*
> *c. Like no other person.*
> *Kluckhohn and Murray (1948)*

Note

I would like to thank my colleague Dr. Ziad Zennie for his valuable comments on this article, and for conducting a good number of interviews for this study.

References

Introduction

Bennis, W. with Biederman, P. W. (2009), *The Essential Bennis*, San Francisco: Jossey-Bass.

Bennis, W. (1989), *On Becoming a Leader*, New York: Addison Wesley.

de Bono, E. (1985), *Tactics: The Art and Science of Success*, London: Fontana/ Collins.

Gladwell, M. (2008), *Outliers: The Story of Success*, New York: Little, Brown and Company.

Goleman, D., Boyatzis, R., and McKee, A. (2002), *Primal Leadership: Realizing the Power of Emotional Intelligence*, Boston: Harvard Business School Press.

Hofstede, G. (2001), *Culture's Consequences: Comparing Values, Behaviors, Institutions, and Organizations Across Nations*, 2nd edn, Thousand Oaks: Sage Publications.

House, R. J., Hanges, P. J., Javidan, M., Dorfman, P. W., and Gupta, V. (eds.) (2004), *Culture, Leadership, and Organizations: The GLOBE Study of 62 Societies*, Thousand Oaks: Sage Publications.

Meirc Training & Consulting (1989), *The Making of Gulf Managers*, unpublished study distributed to Meirc's clients who sponsored the research.

Muna, F. A. (1980), *The Arab Executive*, London: Macmillan Press.

Chapter 1   On Leadership, Followership, and Culture

Bennis, W. and Nanus, B. (1985), *Leaders: The Strategies for Taking Charge*, New York: Harper & Row.

Bennis, W. with Biederman, P. W. (2009), *The Essential Bennis*, San Francisco: Jossey-Bass.

George, B. and Sims, P. (2007), *True North: Discover Your Authentic Leadership*, San Francisco: Jossey-Bass.

Ghemawat, P. (2007), *Redefining Global Strategy: Crossing Borders in a World Where Differences Still Matter*, Boston: Harvard Business School Press.

Hofstede, G. (2001), *Culture's Consequences: Comparing Values, Behaviors, Institutions, and Organizations Across Nations*, 2nd edn, Thousand Oaks: Sage Publications.

House, R. J., Hanges, P. J., Javidan, M., Dorfman, P. W., and Gupta, V. (eds.) (2004), *Culture, Leadership, and Organizations: The GLOBE Study of 62 Societies*, Thousand Oaks: Sage Publications.

Jackson, B. and Parry, K. (2008), *A Very Short, Fairly Interesting and Reasonably Cheap Book About Studying Leadership*, London: Sage Publications.

Kelley, R. E. (1988), "In Praise of Followers," *Harvard Business Review*, Vol. 66, No. 6, pp. 142–8.

Kelley, R. E. (2008), "Rethinking Followership," in R. E. Riggio, I. Chaleff and J. Lipman-Blumen (eds.), *The Art of Followership: How Great Followers Create Great Leaders and Organizations*, San Francisco: Jossey-Bass.

Muna, F. A. and Mansour, N. (2009), "Balancing Work with Personal Life: The Leader as Acrobat," *Journal of Management Development*, Vol. 28, No. 4, pp. 121–33.

Nakata, C. (ed.) (2009), *Beyond Hofstede: Culture Frameworks for Global Marketing and Management*, Basingstoke: Palgrave Macmillan.

Nash, L. and Stevenson, H. (2004), *Just Enough: Tools for Creating Success in Your Work and Life*, New York: John Wiley & Sons.

O'Toole, J. (1995), *Leading Change*, San Francisco: Jossey-Bass.

Chapter 2 A Framework for Understanding Leadership Success

Bennis, W. with Biederman, P. W. (2009), *The Essential Bennis*, San Francisco: Jossey-Bass.

Bennis, W. (1989), *On Becoming a Leader*, New York: Addison Wesley.

Boyatzis, R. (1982), *The Competent Manager: A Model for Effective Performance*, New York: John Wiley & Sons.

Burns, J. M. (1978), *Leadership*, New York: Harper & Row.

de Bono, E. (1985), *Tactics: The Art and Science of Success*, London: Fontana/Collins.

George, B. and Sims, P. (2007), *True North: Discover Your Authentic Leadership*, San Francisco: Jossey-Bass.

Gladwell, M. (2008), *Outliers: The Story of Success*, New York: Little, Brown and Company.

Goldman, E. (2007), "Strategic Thinking at the Top," *MIT Sloan Management Review*, Vol. 48, No. 4, pp. 75–81.

Goleman, D., Boyatzis, R. and McKee, A. (2002), *Primal Leadership: Realizing the Power of Emotional Intelligence*, Boston: Harvard Business School Press.

Handy, C. (1996), *Beyond Certainty: The Changing Worlds of Organizations*, Boston: Harvard Business School Press.

McClelland, D. C. (1973), "Testing for Competence Rather Than for 'Intelligence,'" *American Psychologist*, 28, pp. 1–14.

Meirc Training & Consulting (1989), *The Making of Gulf Managers*, unpublished study distributed to Meirc's clients who sponsored the research.

Muna, F. A. (1980), *The Arab Executive*, London: Macmillan Press.

Muna, F. A. (2003), *Seven Metaphors on Management: Tools for Managers in the Arab World*, Aldershot: Gower Publishing Company.

Sloan, J. (2006), *Learning to Think Strategically*, Burlington, MA: Butterworth-Heinemann.

Chapter 3   A Road Map to Success

Bennis, W. with Biederman, P. W. (2009), *The Essential Bennis*, San Francisco: Jossey-Bass.

Collins, J. and Porras, J. (1994), *Built to Last: Successful Habits of Visionary Companies*, New York: HarperCollins Publishers.

Joyce, W., Nohria, N., and Roberson, B. (2003), *What Really Works: The 4 + 2 Formula for Sustained Business Success*, New York: HarperCollins Publishers.

Ulrich, D., Smallwood, N., and Sweetman, K. (2008), *The Leadership Code: Five Rules to Lead By*, Boston: Harvard Business Press.

Chapter 4   The Early Years of Potential Leaders

Harvard Business Review (2001), "Personal Histories: Leaders Remember the Moments and People that Shaped Them," Vol. 79, No. 11, pp. 27–38.

Meirc Training & Consulting (1989), *The Making of Gulf Managers*, unpublished study distributed to Meirc's clients who sponsored the research.

Muna, F. A. (2003), *Seven Metaphors on Management: Tools for Managers in the Arab World*, Aldershot: Gower Publishing Company.

Chapter 5   Paths to Outstanding Leadership

Bennis, W. (1989), *On Becoming a Leader*, New York: Addison Wesley.

Bennis, W. (2004), "The Seven Ages of the Leader," *Harvard Business Review*, Vol. 82, No. 1, pp. 46–53.

Collins, J. (2001), *Good to Great: Why Some Companies Make the Leap ... and Others Don't*, New York: HarperCollins Publishers.

Covey, S. R. (1989), *The 7 Habits of Highly Effective People*, New York: Simon and Schuster.

Drucker, P. F. (1999), "Managing Oneself," *Harvard Business Review*, Vol. 77, No. 2, pp. 65–74.

Hall, E. (1971), *Beyond Culture*, New York: Anchor/Doubleday.

Hofstede, G. (2001), *Culture's Consequences: Comparing Values, Behavior, Institutions and Organizations across Nations*, 2nd edn, Thousand Oaks: Sage Publications.

Kambil, A., Long, V. W., and Kwan, C. (2006), "The Seven Disciplines for Venturing in China," *MIT Sloan Management Review*, Vol. 47, No. 2, pp. 85–9.

LeBaron, M. (2003), *Bridging Cultural Conflicts: New Approaches for a Changing World*, San Francisco: Jossey-Bass.

Mintzberg, H. (2004), *Managers not MBAs*, San Francisco: Berrett-Koehler Publishers.

Meirc Training & Consulting (1989), *The Making of Gulf Managers*, unpublished study distributed to Meirc's clients who sponsored the research.

Muna, F. A. (2003), *Seven Metaphors on Management: Tools for Managers in the Arab World*, Aldershot: Gower Publishing Company.

Trompenaars, F. and Hamden-Turner, C. (1997), *Riding the Waves of Culture*, 2nd edn, New York: McGraw-Hill.

Ulrich, D., Smallwood, N., and Sweetman, K. (2008), *The Leadership Code: Five Rules to Lead By*, Boston: Harvard Business Press.

Welch, J. (2005), *Winning*, NY: HarperCollins Publishers.

Wheatcroft, A. J. M. and Hawatmeh, C. Z. (2008), *A Promised Fulfilled: Elia Costandi Nuqul and His Business Odyssey*, London: I. B. Tauris.

Chapter 6 Learning to Lead: Cultivating Emotional Intelligence

Ali, A. J. (2005), *Islamic Perspectives on Management and Organization*, Cheltenham: Edward Elgar Publishing.

Andersen, P. A., Hecht, M. L., Hoobler, G. D., and Smallwood, M. (2004), "Nonverbal Communication Across Culture," in W. B. Guykunst (ed.), *Cross-Cultural and Intercultural Communication*, Thousand Oaks: Sage Publications.

Bennis, W., Goleman, D., and O'Toole, J. (2008), *Transparency: How Leaders Create a Culture of Candor*, San Francisco: Jossey-Bass.

Bennis, W. with Biederman, P. W. (2009), *The Essential Bennis*, San Francisco: Jossey-Bass.

Boyatzis, R. (1982), *The Competent Manager: A Model for Effective Performance*, New York: John Wiley & Sons.

Boyatzis, R. E. and Ratti, F. (2009), "Emotional, Social and Cognitive Intelligence Competencies Distinguishing Effective Italian Managers and Executives in a Private Company and Cooperatives," *Journal of Management Development*, Vol. 28, No. 9, pp. 821–38.

Buckingham, M. (2005), "What Great Managers Do," *Harvard Business Review*, Vol. 83, No. 3, pp. 103–11.

Buckingham, M. (2007), *Go Put Your Strengths to Work: 6 Powerful Steps to Achieve Outstanding Performance*, New York: Free Press.

Caruso, D. R. and Salovey, P. (2004), *The Emotionally Intelligent Manager: How to Develop and Use the Four Key Emotional Skills of Leadership*, San Francisco: Jossey-Bass.

Caruso, D. R. (2008), "Emotions and the Ability Model of Emotional Intelligence," in Emmerling, R. J., Shanwal, V. K., and Mandal, M. K. (eds.), *Emotional Intelligence: Theoretical and Cultural Perspectives*, NY: Nova Science Publishers.

Drucker, P. F. (1999), "Managing Oneself," *Harvard Business Review*, Vol. 77, No. 2, pp. 65–74.

Gardner, H. (1983), *Frames of Mind: The Theory of Multiple Intelligences*, New York: Basic Books.

George B., Sims, P., McLean, A. N., and Mayer, D. (2007), "Discovering Your Authentic Leadership," *Harvard Business Review*, New York: Vol. 85, No. 2, pp. 129–38.

Ghorbani, N., Bing, M. N., Watson, P. J., Davison, H. K., and Mark, D. A. (2002), "Self-Reported Emotional Intelligence: Construct Similarity and

Functional Dissimilarity of Higher-Order Processing in Iran and the United States," *International Journal of Psychology*, Vol. 37, No. 5, pp. 297–308.

Goleman, D. (1995), *Emotional Intelligence: Why It Can Matter More Than IQ*, New York: Bantam Books.

Goleman, D., Boyatzis, R., and McKee, A. (2002), *Primal Leadership: Realizing the Power of Emotional Intelligence*, Boston: Harvard Business School Press.

Kouzes, J. M. and Posner, B. Z. (1995), *The Leadership Challenge: How to Keep Getting Extraordinary Things Done in Organizations*, 2nd edn, San Francisco: Jossey-Bass.

Mayer, J. D. and Salovey, P. (1997), "What is Emotional Intelligence?," in P. Salovey, and D. Sluyter (eds.), *Emotional Development and Emotional Intelligence: Implications for Educators*, New York: Basic Book.

McClelland, D. C. (1973), "Testing for Competence Rather than for Intelligence," *American Psychologist*, Vol. 28, No. 1, January, pp. 1–14.

Muna, F. A. (1980), *The Arab Executive*, London: Macmillan Press.

Muna, F. A. (2003), *Seven Metaphors on Management: Tools for Managers in the Arab World*, Aldershot: Gower Publishing Company.

O'Toole, J. and Bennis, W. (2009), "What's Needed Next: A Culture of Candor," *Harvard Business Review*, Vol. 87, No. 6, pp. 54–61.

Sharma, R. (2006), *The Greatness Guide: Powerful Secrets for Getting to World Class*, New York: HarperCollins Publishers.

Scherer, K. R. and Walbott, H. G. (1994), "Evidence for Universality and Cultural Variation of Differential Emotion Response Patterning," *Journal of Personality and Social Psychology*, 66, 310–28.

Spencer, L. M. and Spencer, S. M. (1993), *Competence at Work: Models for Superior Performance*, New York: John Wiley & Sons.

Chapter 7   Styles of Emotionally Intelligent Leaders

Dickson, M. W., Den Hartog, D. N., and Mitchelson, J. (2003), "Research on Leadership in a Cross-Cultural Context: Making Progress, and Raising New Questions," *The Leadership Quarterly*, Vol. 14, No. 6, pp. 729–68.

Goleman, D., Boyatzis, R., and McKee, A. (2002), *Primal Leadership: Realizing the Power of Emotional Intelligence*, Boston: Harvard Business School Press.

Goleman, D. (2000), "Leadership that Gets Results," *Harvard Business Review*, March–April, Vol. 78, No. 2, pp. 78–90.

House, R. J., Hanges, P. J., Javidan, M., Dorfman, P. W., and Gupta, V. (eds.) (2004), *Culture, Leadership, and Organizations: The GLOBE Study of 62 Societies*, Thousand Oaks: Sage Publications.

Chapter 8   Decision-Making Styles, Execution, and Accountability

Alexander, J. (2007), *Performance Dashboards and Analysis for Value Creation*, Hoboken, NJ: John Wiley & Sons.

Ali, A. J. (2005), *Islamic Perspectives on Management and Organization*, Cheltenham, UK: Edward Elgar Publishing.

Ali, A. J. and Schaupp, D. (1992), "Value Systems as Predictors of Managerial Decision Making Styles of Arab Executives," *International Journal of Manpower*, Vol. 13, No. 3, pp. 19–26.

Bossidy, L. and Charan, R. (2002), *Execution: The Discipline of Getting Things Done*, NY: Crown Business.

Collins, J. (2001), *Good to Great: Why Some Companies Make the Leap ... and Others Don't*, New York: HarperCollins Publishers.

Drucker, P. F. (1967), *The Effective Executive*, New York: Harper & Row.

Hammer, M. (2007), "The 7 Deadly Sins of Performance Measurement and How to Avoid Them," *MIT Sloan Management Review*, Vol. 48, No. 3, pp. 19–28.

Hewlett, S. A. and Rashid, R. (2010), "The Battle for Female Talent in Emerging Markets," *Harvard Business Review*, Vol. 88, No. 5, May, pp. 101–6.

Hofstede, G. (2001), *Culture's Consequences: Comparing Values, Behaviors, Institutions, and Organizations Across Nations*, 2nd edn, Thousand Oaks: Sage Publications.

Hofstede, G. (2010), the quote is from http://www.geert-hofstede.com/, date accessed March 3, 2010.

Huselid, M. A., Becker, B. E., and Beatty, R. W. (2005), *The Workforce Scorecard: Managing Human Capital to Execute Strategy*, Boston: Harvard Business School Press.

Kaplan, R. S. and Norton, D. P. (2008), *The Execution Premium: Linking Strategy to Operations for Competitive Advantage*, Boston: Harvard Business School Press.

Kim, W. C. and Mauborgne, R. (2005), *Blue Ocean Strategy: How to Create Uncontested Market Space and Make the Competition Irrelevant*, Boston: Harvard Business School Press.

Miles, R. H. (2010), "Accelerating Corporate Transformations," *Harvard Business Review*, Vol. 88, No. 1, January–February 2010, pp. 69–75.

Miner, J. B. (2005), *Organizational Behavior: Essential Theories of Motivation and Leadership*, New York: M. E. Sharpe, Inc.

Meirc Training & Consulting (1989), *The Making of Gulf Managers*, unpublished study distributed to Meirc's clients who sponsored the research.

Muna, F. A. (1980), *The Arab Executive*, London: Macmillan Press.

Muna, F. A. (2003), *Seven Metaphors on Management: Tools for Managers in the Arab World*, Aldershot: Gower Publishing Company.

Muna, F. A. (forthcoming 2012), "Contextual Leadership: A Study of Lebanese Executives Working in Lebanon, the GCC Countries, and the United States," *Journal of Management Development*, Vol. 31, No. 1.

Roberto, M. A. (2005), *Why Great Leaders Don't Take Yes for an Answer: Managing for Conflict and Consensus*, New Jersey: Wharton School Publishing.

Ulrich, D., Smallwood, N., and Sweetman, K. (2008), *The Leadership Code: Five Rules to Lead By*, Boston: Harvard Business Press.

Vinnicombe, S. and Bank, J. (2003), *Women with Attitude: Lessons for Career Management*, London: Routledge.

Vroom, V. H. and Jago, A. G. (1988), *The New Leadership: Managing Participation in Organizations*, New York: Prentice Hall.

Vroom, V. H. (2000), "Leadership and the Decision-Making Process," *Organizational Dynamics*, Vol. 28, No. 4, pp. 82–94.

Yousef, D. A. (1998), "Predictors of Decision-Making Styles in a Non-Western Country," *Leadership & Organization Development Journal*, Vol. 19, No. 7, pp. 366–73.

Chapter 9   Recruiting and Developing Talent

Becker, B. E., Huselid, M. A., and Beatty, R. W. (2009), *The Differentiated Workforce: Transforming Talent into Strategic Impact*, Boston: Harvard Business Press.

Bossidy, L. (2001), "The Job No CEO Should Delegate," *Harvard Business Review*, Vol. 79, No. 3, pp. 46–9.

Collins, J. (2001), *Good to Great: Why Some Companies Make the Leap ... and Others Don't*, New York: HarperCollins Publishers.

Fernandez-Araoz, C., Groysberg, B., and Nohria, N. (2009), "The Definitive Guide to Recruiting in Good Times and Bad," *Harvard Business Review*, Vol. 87, No. 5, pp. 74–84.

Ghemawat, P. (2010), "Finding Your Strategy in the New Landscape," *Harvard Business Review*, Vol. 88, No. 3, March 2001, pp. 54–60.

Kotter, J. P. (2001), "What Leaders Really Do," *Harvard Business Review*, Vol. 79, No 11, pp. 85–97.

McCall, M. W. (2007), "Every Strength a Weakness," a paper given at the Annual Meeting of the Society for Industrial and Organizational Psychology, held in New York City, on April 27, 2007. Available online at: http://www.kaplandevries.com/images/uploads/EveryStrengthWeakness_McCallSIOP07.pdf, date accessed February 25, 2010.

McCall, M. W. and Hollenbeck, G. P. (2002), *Developing Global Executives: The Lessons of International Experience*, Boston: Harvard Business School Press.

Muna, F. A. (2004), "Cultivating HR: The Leader as Gardener," *Organisations & People*, Vol. 11, No. 3, pp. 18–26.

Sample, S. B. (2002), *The Contrarian's Guide to Leadership*, San Francisco: Jossey-Bass.

Welch, J. (2005), *Winning*, New York: HarperCollins Publishers.

Chapter 10   Final Thoughts

Bennis, W. (1989), *On Becoming a Leader*, New York: Addison Wesley.

Bennis, W. and O'Toole, J. (2005), "How Business Schools Lost Their Way", *Harvard Business Review*, May 2005.

Boyatzis, R. E. and Ratti, F. (2009), "Emotional, Social and Cognitive Intelligence Competencies Distinguishing Effective Italian Managers and Executives in a Private Company and Cooperatives," *Journal of Management Development*, Vol. 28, No. 9, pp. 821–38.

Farson, R. and Keys, R. (2002), "The Failure-Tolerant Leader," *Harvard Business Review*, August 2002, Vol. 80, No. 8, pp. 64–71.

Friedman, T. (2005), *The World is Flat: A Brief History of the Twenty-First Century*, New York: Farrar, Straus and Giroux.

Ghemawat, P. (2010), "Finding Your Strategy in the New Landscape," *Harvard Business Review*, Vol. 88, No. 3, March 2010, pp. 54–60.

Ghemawat, P. (2011), "The Cosmopolitan Corporation," *Harvard Business Review*, Vol. 89, No. 5, May 2011, pp. 92–9.

Goleman, D., Boyatzis, R. and McKee, A. (2002), *Primal Leadership: Realizing the Power of Emotional Intelligence*, Boston: Harvard Business School Press.

Hofstede, G. (2001), *Culture's Consequences: Comparing Values, Behaviors, Institutions, and Organizations Across Nations*, 2nd edn, Thousand Oaks: Sage Publications.

Hofstede, G. and Hofstede, G. J. (2005), *Cultures and Organizations: Software of the Mind*, 2nd edn, New York: McGraw-Hill.

House, R. J., Hanges, P. J., Javidan, M., Dorfman, P. W., and Gupta, V. (eds.), (2004), *Culture, Leadership, and Organizations: The GLOBE Study of 62 Societies*, Thousand Oaks: Sage Publications.

Khurana, R. and Nohria, N. (2008), "It's Time to Make Management a True Profession," *Harvard Business Review*, Vol. 86, No. 10, pp. 70–7.

McCall, M. W. and Hollenbeck, G. P. (2002), *Developing Global Executives: The Lessons of International Experience*, Boston: Harvard Business School Press.

Mintzberg, H. (2004), *Managers not MBAs: A Look at the Soft Practice of Managing and Management Development*, San Francisco: Berrett-Koehler Publishers.

Meirc Training & Consulting (1989), *The Making of Gulf Managers*, unpublished study distributed to Meirc's clients who sponsored the research.

Muna, F. A. (1980), *The Arab Executive*, London: Macmillan Press.

Muna, F. A. (2003), *Seven Metaphors on Management: Tools for Managers in the Arab World*, Aldershot: Gower Publishing Company.

Muna, F. A. (forthcoming 2012), "Contextual Leadership: A Study of Lebanese Executives Working in Lebanon, the GCC Countries, and the United States," *Journal of Management Development*, Vol. 31, No. 1.

Nakata, C., ed. (2009), *Beyond Hofstede: Culture Frameworks for Global Marketing and Management*, Basingstoke: Palgrave Macmillan.

Podolny, J. M. (2009a), "The Buck Stops (and Starts) at Business Schools," *Harvard Business Review*, Vol. 87, No. 6, pp. 62–7.

Podolny, J. M. (2009b), "Joel M. Podolny, 'How Business Schools Lost Their Way,'" in Bennis, *The Essential Bennis*, San Francisco: Jossey-Bass.

Welch, J. (2005), *Winning*, New York: HarperCollins Publishers.

Appendix C   The Extended Study of Lebanese Executives

Ali, A. J. (2005), *Islamic Perspectives on Management and Organization*, Cheltenham: Edward Elgar Publishing.

Becht, B. (2010), "Building a Company Without Borders", *Harvard Business Review*, April 2010, Vo. 88, No. 4, pp. 103–6.

Bennis, W. (2009), *The Essential Bennis*, San Francisco, CA: Jossey-Bass.

Dickson, M. W., Den Hartog, D. N., and Mitchelson, J. K. (2003), "Research on Leadership in a Cross-Cultural Context: Making Progress, and Raising New Questions," *The Leadership Quarterly*, Vol. 14, No. 6, pp. 729–68.

Dickson, M. W., Den Hartog, D. N., and Castaño, N. (2009), "Understanding Leadership Across Cultures," in R. S. Bhagat and R. M. Steers (eds), *Cambridge Handbook of Culture, Organizations, and Work*, Cambridge: Cambridge University Press.

Ghemawat, P. (2007), *Redefining Global Strategy: Crossing Borders in a World Where Differences Still Matter*, Boston, MA: Harvard Business School Press.

Goleman, D. (1995), *Emotional Intelligence: Why it Can Matter More Than IQ*, New York, NY: Bantam Books.

Goleman, D., Boyatzis, R. and McKee, A. (2002), *Primal Leadership: Realizing the Power of Emotional Intelligence*, Boston, MA: Harvard Business School Press.

Hofstede, G. (1980), *Culture's Consequences: International Differences on Work-Related Values*, London: Sage Publications.

Hofstede, G. (2001), *Culture's Consequences: Comparing Values, Behaviors, Institutions, and Organizations Across Nations*, 2nd edn, Thousand Oaks, CA: Sage Publications.

House, R. J., Hanges, P. J., Javidan, M., Dorfman, P. W., and Gupta, V. (eds), (2004), *Culture, Leadership, and Organizations: The GLOBE Study of 62 Societies*, Thousand Oaks, CA: Sage Publications.

Ilangovan, A., Scroggins, W. A., and Rozell, E. J. (2007), "Managerial Perspectives on Emotional Intelligence Differences between India and the United States: The Development of Research Propositions," *International Journal of Management*, Vol. 24, No. 3, pp. 541–8.

Jackson, B. and Parry, K. (2008), *A Very Short, Fairly Interesting and Reasonably Cheap Book About Studying Leadership*, London: Sage Publications.

Javidan, M., House, R. J., Dorfman, P. W., Hanges, P. J., and Sully de Luque, M. (2006), "Conceptualizing and Measuring Cultures and their Consequences: a Comparative Review of GLOBE's and Hofstede's Approaches," *Journal of International Business Studies*, Vol. 37, No. 6, pp. 897–914.

Leung, A. S. M. (2005), "Emotional Intelligence or Emotional Blackmail: A Study of a Chinese Professional Service Firm," *International Journal of Cross-Cultural Management*, Vol. 5, No. 2, pp. 181–96.

McCall, M. W. and Hollenbeck, G. P. (2002), *Developing Global Executives: The Lessons of International Experience*, Boston, MA: Harvard Business School Press.

Meirc Training & Consulting (1989), *The Making of Gulf Managers*, a research study published by Meirc for companies that sponsored the research.

Muna, F. A. (1980), *The Arab Executive*, London: Macmillan Press.

Muna, F. A. (2003), *Seven Metaphors on Management: Tools for Managers in the Arab World*, Aldershot: Gower Publishing.

Muna, F. A. and Zennie, Z. A. (2010), *Developing Multicultural Leaders: The Journey to Leadership Success*, Basingstoke: Palgrave Macmillan.

Nakata, C. (2009), (ed.), *Beyond Hofstede: Culture Frameworks for Global Marketing and Management*, Basingstoke: Palgrave Macmillan.

Nardon, L. and Steers, R. M. (2009), "The Culture Theory Jungle: Divergence and Convergence in Models of National Cultures", in R. S. Bhagat, and R. M. Steers, (eds), *Cambridge Handbook of Culture, Organizations, and Work*, Cambridge: Cambridge University Press.

Roberts, K. H. (1970), "On Looking at an Elephant: An Evaluation of Cross-Cultural Research Related to Organizations," *Psychological Bulletin*, Vol. 74, No. 4, pp. 327–50.

Thomas, R. J. (2008), *Crucibles of Leadership: How to Learn from Experience to Become a Great Leader*, Boston, MA: Harvard Business School Press.

Vroom, V. H. (2000), "Leadership and the Decision-Making Process," *Organizational Dynamics*, Vol. 28, No. 4, pp. 82–94.

Yahchouchi, G. (2009), "Employees' Perceptions of Lebanese Managers' Leadership Style and Organizational Commitment," *International Journal of Leadership Studies*, Vol. 4, No. 2, pp. 127–40.

Index